Table

Introduction..........................
Who Am I? 3
What Does Nature Got to Do with it? 11
Leading to My Discovery of the Circle Theory 13
The Circle Theory 17
Polarity: Creating Limitations in Your Life 27
Does Judgment Hold You Hostage? 31
Allowance: Expanding the Possibility of You and Your Life 35
Invalidating Others' Points of View 39
The Center of the Circle – Do you have an Agenda? 45
The Illusion of Positivity 51
Empowerment of Perspective 53
When Judgement Triggers you 55
The Power of a Question 59
Introduction to Energy 61
Energetic Barriers 65
Become Undefinable and Choosing Beyond the Circle .. 69
Mind, Body, Soul, and Spirit 73
Connection 81
Do You Value You? 85
My Gift to You 89
Acknowledgements 91
Appendix A 93
    Using the Circle 93
Appendix B 95
    Listing of various Alternative Therapies & reference material: .. 95
Appendix C 97
    Summary of the Questions for Ponder & Self Discovery 97

THE
ART OF
CHOOSING
YOU

*Geri,
The more you choose you — the more you invite others to choose you!
Robin Chant*

TOOLS TO RADICALLY SHIFT YOUR LIFE

Robin Chant

Edited by Helena Morales

 FriesenPress

Suite 300 - 990 Fort St
Victoria, BC, V8V 3K2
Canada

www.friesenpress.com

Copyright © 2020 by Robin Chant
First Edition — 2020

Edited by Helena Morales & Joanne Johnston

This is a book to invite you to step out of judgment and step more into being you. Judgment does not have to rule your life, you can rule your life. I invite you to go beyond judgment to create a life beyond your wildest dreams.

All rights reserved.

No part of this publication may be reproduced in any form, or by any means, electronic or mechanical, including photocopying, recording, or any information browsing, storage, or retrieval system, without permission in writing from FriesenPress.

ISBN
978-1-5255-6634-9 (Hardcover)
978-1-5255-6635-6 (Paperback)
978-1-5255-6636-3 (eBook)

1. SELF-HELP, MOTIVATIONAL & INSPIRATIONAL

Distributed to the trade by The Ingram Book Company

*There are times in our lives when we have chosen to be pathetic
and times when we have chosen to be brilliant.
None of those times define us.
Our goal in this life is to embody
any one of the many possible characteristics when
the moment requires it and to not judge it.*

Introduction

The Art of Choosing you is a roadmap to rediscovering you, the you, you were before you let judgement stop you. It is a resource to help you to become the person you knew you wanted to be. It delves into the heart of you and awakens the person that has been sleeping through life. It is a powerful book that guides you through the steps to reignite your potency and truly become the infinite being you are. It examines the effect of judgements and the trap we fall into. It opens up possibilities and teaches you to embrace the connection with your mind, body, spirit and soul. It takes you on a journey of discovering how you set limitations on yourself and others. It teaches you about allowance and how to empower you and value yourself. It changes your perspective of this reality.

How often do you think you judge yourself? If you never judged yourself again and no one ever judged you again, would there be more in your life that you would choose to be and do? There are many reasons why we may choose to judge; to feel safe, to fit in with those around us, or to stand against society or it could purely be subconscious. Are you willing to look at what judgment actually is? If we are judging something in our lives as negative or positive, are we using judgment as a source for our creating our lives? Are we truly seeing what is there or are we seeing it through the eyes of judgment? Where does this judgment lead us? It leads us to the polarity of right and wrong, of good and bad. We are in constant battle in our minds as we focus on this polarity. Are we addicted to making ourselves or others right or wrong? I am inviting you to start creating your life and yourself without judgment. Would you like to let go of the habit of judgment and choose *allowance* instead?

Throughout this book, I use the word "allowance" to mean the state of refraining from forming a judgment, a state of freedom. This usage may seem unfamiliar, but I find it to be the best way to express this idea. A similar and perhaps more familiar concept is "permission," but that word suggests an acceptance of judgment rather than its absence. The idea is that, if we can be in allowance of everything being an interesting point of view, we no longer need to be motivated to prove either for or against said judgment, and can rather be inspired by our own true desires.

What would our lives be like if we were able to choose allowance for ourselves and others? I desire to see a world where judgment does not determine what we choose —where we can choose ourselves and the lives we create beyond judgement. When we choose allowance, rather than opting against negativity or for positivity, we can create the art of choosing ourselves.

If you are always trying to be positive, does that give you a chance to be you in totality? If you are avoiding the negative, are you living fully?

I created this book to invite you to look at what judgment does to you and how it locks you into a life of limitations. I invite you to choose allowance—to allow you and your life to be something greater. Allowance is how you get to be you and how others get to be themselves with no requirement to change anything.

Who Am I?

One of the questions people most think about and ask themselves—whether they do it consciously or unconsciously—is, "Who am I?" Most of the time our answer is the career or job we have chosen to pursue, or the roles we have identified with: "I am a firefighter/lawyer/doctor/mother." Yet, any one of those is not who we are completely. We use these jobs, roles, or titles to try and define ourselves. This, however, limits us in how we are perceived by ourselves and others, and simultaneously leaves us seeking to continually define ourselves.

The only question that really matters is: Who am I? Many of us spend our entire lives trying to figure this out. Are we what our parents and society tell us we should be? Do we ignore this question, so it does not confuse us from who we think we are? What defines us? Is it through our choices in our lives that we become who we are or is there something else that defines us? Not everyone enjoys making choices, for what if we make the wrong choice? How do we know what the right choice is and is that what really defines us? Some people feel that the fewer choices they face, the better the chance of making the right choices. Who decides, though, what is right or what is wrong for us?

As I was approaching adulthood, many people in my community, my friends and family, were trying to get me to choose the "right" relationship, settle down, get married, and have children. I must admit that it confused me, for I believed that all this was optional, but no one was honouring me for exercising my own choices. Settling down and raising children seemed to be in the script that society has given us, and we may feel we must follow the script without actually choosing it. Were you present in your choices while you were growing up? Were you honoured in your choices? Or did you choose based on what others desired for you? Do you honour others in their choices if they differ from yours? Choice is preferring one thing over another. If we do not know our desires, then it is difficult to choose based on our own preferences and then we will likely allow others to influence our choices in life.

The people in my life never considered the possibility that marriage and children did not fit me, even when I told them. They could not fathom the idea not of marriage and having children as optional. They kept telling me things like, "Everyone has to have children; that is what you do, especially as a woman," or, "Oh, you think that now, but one day you will change your mind." They could not hear me or understand my choices because it was not how they understood the world to be. These concepts were not optional in their world and realities. They were raised to believe that all women should be married with children, and that there was probably something wrong with those who did not or could not. In their eyes, I was broken, and they needed to fix me. I did not know how to relate to them, because even though I was not inherently against marriage or raising children, it just did not resonate with me. My view went against what society was telling me I should desire, and it seemed to be all they ever talked about. I felt like they would not really be able to see me and that I would not be validated unless I adapted to their idea of what a woman should be and do. This created conflict with my inner self and my outer world. I felt alone. I felt I could not make meaningful connections, so I kept myself and my inner desires hidden from most people. Do you allow yourself to get in touch with your inner desires, or are you keeping your inner desires secret from yourself and from others?

We have hearts and minds; our minds try to make sense and logic out of a given situation, whereas the heart just knows what it wants. When our minds do not match our hearts' desires, we often create conflict within ourselves. To honour what was in my heart, my inner wisdom, I knew I had to choose a life without kids or marriage. But in my mind, I was wrong for wanting something other than what was in the script—wrong in the eyes of society, my family, and my friends; there was something wrong with me for not being happy with what others wanted for me. My mind was trying to understand *why* I did not want what everyone else seemed to want. I made their judgment of me my judgment. I was in my head, but all the while my heart kept telling me to choose differently. My heart and mind were in a constant battle. If I had followed my head, I would not have made the choices I did and would not be who I am today. I would have had children to fit in and be like everyone else. I would have given up what I knew to be true for me for the sake of others. How often have you chosen to go against your heart and what it desires so that you will not be judged by others? Choosing what my heart knew to be true for me went against what others had in mind for me—it even cost me some friendships—but I had to choose it for me. Are you willing to choose what your heart desires for you?

If I had chosen, against my heart, to live a life of being married, would my spouse have felt the effects eventually? Would my children have felt that my deepest desire was to be free, without fully being there for them? Would the conflict between my heart and my mind spill over into my environment, creating conflict around me? Would my spouse and kids see how I achingly longed for a different life? I probably would have made the best of it while at the same time going into a depression because I was limiting what I truly desired. I sense that going against what one truly desire is a big contributing factor to depression.

As I entered adulthood, I had to plan for what I was going to do to create money flow in my life. Twenty-five years ago, a job was stereotypically viewed as either a "man's job" or a "woman's job." Firefighter positions were predominantly held by men and considered a "man's job." By choosing to work with mostly males, I believed it would relieve the pressure I felt of what others thought I needed to be. I decided on "a man's job"—to be a firefighter—thinking it would solve a lot of my problems. Fire did not scare me, I could drive the large trucks, and I was used to hanging out with men. I had grown up loving farm work and being with my dad. At the time, choosing to be a firefighter met all the criteria on my list of what I would need to be a self-sustaining, happy woman. In this job, I could make a "man's" wage to support myself while at the same time prove to myself and everyone else that I did not need to have a spouse or children to fulfill my life.

I was unconsciously surrounding myself with people that would not judge me for choosing to be without children or a spouse. Over the years, a few of the men I worked with, made me wrong for not having a spouse or children, but most were in allowance of my choices without question. Alternatively, I found it increasingly hard to hang out with other women, for almost all the women in my community would question and judge me and my choices. Do you judge others negatively when you do not understand their choices? What would it be like if we honoured others' choices whether we understood them or not? Do you try to make your choices match others'?

I grew in my career and came to identify myself only as a firefighter. The more I attempted to prove I was a capable, functioning, well-rounded individual on my own, the more I realized something was missing. I was coming out to the world as me—child-free and spouse-free—and yet I was not happy. I began to wonder if my choices were creating my unhappiness. I was going for what I desired, yet it did not bring me the happiness I thought it would. I could not figure out what was missing. Should I have chosen a life with marriage and children as everyone around me was doing? Was not having children the missing element in my life? I was lost and confused even though I was following what my heart desired.

I did not realize that I had the choice to be so much more than my career—to be all of me. I had not realized that being a firefighter, and being child-free, spouse-free, and independent, were just parts of me. That identity was not all of me; no wonder I was going more deeply into depression. I did not recognize that I had the choice to be greater, to be more, and I did not need to identify or define myself as a certain something.

The more I defined myself as a certain "something", the more I tried to hide other parts of me that did not match this definition. Whenever I would express joy from being around children, people would equate that joy with a responsibility to bear children and treat it like the missing element for what would truly make my life complete. They would make my choice wrong and push me to comply with their own beliefs that having children was the only way to experience true joy. It was as if, to them, experiencing joy and having children were inseparable.

I truly liked children but had no desire to have my own children. Every time I expressed joy around children, people around me demanded that I had to have my own children. This felt very oppressive to me and it put me into a bind. In my mind, my only choice was to not show joy around children so that I would not be made wrong for not desiring them in my life. But this then became an important part of myself that I was no longer expressing. Hiding my unexpressed joy around children made me question the decisions I had made, leading to greater inner conflict. I became disconnected from myself, the inner me. It felt like turmoil. This was also at a time when being heterosexual was the only acceptable norm; I wondered if this is what people who identified as gay must go through—they either had to keep it a secret or were treated like it was just a phase that they were supposed to grow out of or "fix". I sympathize; to have to hide such an essential part of yourself is a lonely place of inner conflict. Are you hiding an essential part of you from others?

How many times have we, in our minds, made ourselves wrong for the decisions we made when we were following our hearts? When people seem so opposed to our decisions, the negative judgment can stop us dead in our tracks. By the same token, how many times have we made others wrong for going against what we think is best for them when they are following their own heart?

We learned at a young age to not question authority. We are often expected to not "rock the boat" because doing so would pit us against our families, friends, traditions, or communities. When we find ourselves in resistance to their guidance, it can leave us in conflict or a state of reaction. In reaction, we try to prove others wrong and ourselves right; all the while, we are making these choices based on judgments rather than from a place of authenticity. We get caught up in this cycle of buying other people's projections and expectations of who we are and how we should be. We are never shown how to become our whole, authentic selves because, so few others have any idea what that looks like for them.

If you did grow up with family and friends who supported all your choices, please have gratitude for that; for most of us, knowing what to choose for our lives seemed like a constant battle.

Are we conditioned to be the result of our cultures' designs? We may choose what society says we are supposed to do, or we may choose against society's norms to avoid becoming like everyone else we have observed. Are we aligning and agreeing with what others envision for us without realizing it? Whether we align and agree or resist and react, we are choosing a life based on the experiences of others rather than looking inside ourselves. It may be easier to support others in their choices while failing miserably to do the same for ourselves. Are you willing to honour your choices?

How much energy did I put into trying to prove to everyone else that I was happy with what I had decided? I was missing the point—I had absolutely nothing to prove. Who was I trying to prove it all to? If you are trying to prove anything, you are not in *allowance* of what you truly desire. If you truly desired it, there would be nothing to prove. Do you know what you truly desire?

Do you know in your heart that you are more than your career, title, or role in life? How many of us have gotten lost in our careers or someone else's concept of what we should be, when really, we are looking for meaning in being authentic and whole? Is it possible that by defining ourselves with a career, title, or role, we limit ourselves? Often, as soon as you define yourself it limits you. If you define yourself as a mother you tend to lose the inner sense that you are also much more in addition to that. How much do we limit ourselves by labeling ourselves?

Many of us conform to the path set out by our cultures, traditions, friends, peers, and communities in order to avoid judgment. We adjust so we will fit in. How many times in life have you not chosen something because you were afraid of how you would be judged for it? Sometimes we think it will be easier to avoid taking risks and live with the regrets and all the things we wish we would have done. But what if there was something more than this? What if we took the risk to do what our hearts truly desired? What if we stood out from others? If we are not wanting to stand out from others, what is stopping us? Why is it so scary to stand out? If the answer is judgment, the *circle theory will* help us to see what judgment truly is and how we can get past this roadblock.

We are in the habit of keeping so busy or preoccupied with our "to-do" list that we do not take the time to reflect on these questions that could change everything for us: "Who am I?" and, "What is it that I truly desire?" These questions put forward endless possibilities for how to present ourselves to our families, to our friends, to our communities, and within our own hearts. Creating a life, you truly desire does not have to go against the desires of others. Co-creating with another is in itself a choice. Even co-creating with yourself is a choice. Each choice leads to awareness of new possibilities. Allowing myself more choices in life created greater possibilities for me. I wonder: if we were all to create more possibilities in our lives, what would that create for the world?

The questions in this book are tools that allow you to consider something different in your world. I invite you to look at your life without limitations and to finally start choosing what you truly desire. What we are really exploring is a different way of being. If conforming to society does not appeal to you, what can you do? Does it require radical change? Maybe, maybe not. Do you have to turn your whole world upside-down to find out? What if the turmoil and conflict you are experiencing now *is* the upside-down? What would you choose in your life if judgment was not a factor? What limiting points of view are you willing to let go of to find out? I welcome you to look at everything from a different perspective. Are you willing to step into a world of more choices and possibilities?

What Does Nature Got to Do with it?

Over the years, I have asked people what they desire in life; many respond that they desire the peacefulness of nature. They say that when they walk in nature, they feel peace, and would like to bring that peacefulness into their lives whether they are in nature or not. Now, when you walk in nature and tune into all that is going on around you, is there peace? There is always something growing, something dying, something decomposing—like insects digesting a fallen tree, or one animal hunting another animal to feed its young: it is the circle of life. What brings peace to all of this is that no one part of this circle of life has any point of view or judgment about any other part of the process; it just is what it is. They are in complete allowance of what is happening—with death, destruction, rebirth, and growth. What would your life be like if you were able to choose to be in total allowance of everything happening around you? Nature has no point of view of good or bad or right or wrong; it has total allowance of everything. Just as Nature has its own circle of life that operates in total allowance, I encourage you to join me in looking at another circle that will help to bring peace and allowance into your own world.

The peacefulness we experience in Nature comes from nature's total allowance for everything going on. How peaceful could your life be if you were to choose total allowance for you and every judgment delivered at you?

Leading to My Discovery of the Circle Theory

I found myself going through the motions with friends and acquaintances without any true connection to anyone. My fear of being criticized or dredging up the right and wrong of my choices left me keeping everyone at arm's length. The only thing I knew to do at the time was to coast along and not go too deep, with myself nor with others. I kept busy and did not believe I could have meaningful connections with others for fear of being judged; this also led me to not have a connection with myself. My outside world matched my inside world. None of my friends or family could take away the loneliness I had created for myself. I created this loneliness by not honouring my choices for what they truly were: choices. Instead I wondered what was wrong with me for not wanting the same things. How could I connect with others if they could not understand me? How could they understand me if I did not understand myself?

When it came time to take holidays from work, the idea of going somewhere and spending a solid week with someone that I was not connected to, was not appealing. I did not yet see my aversion to getting to know someone, or letting them get to know me, as an issue; I just chalked it up to being busy. My creative solution that let me sidestep holidays with others was to volunteer everywhere I could to try and help others. Looking back, I can clearly see the irony that I was the one who required help. My inner conflict was at an all-time high. I had yet to meet anyone that appreciated my life choices. I was not even appreciating my life choices. Are you able to appreciate your life choices?

At 29 years of age, I volunteered for the Disaster Relief in Puerto Rico through the Canadian Red Cross. This would be the "TSN® turning point" of my life. There I met Paul, a man who truly honoured the fact that I did not want children in my life. Paul was the first person to give me the space to be okay with my choices; I did not have to defend, deny, second-guess, or prove anything. When I opened up to him, there was so much room to breathe! He gave me the space to be me and did not judge me for my choices. He supported what worked for me in my life and could relate to it. Paul was my age and newly divorced. He and his ex-wife had gotten married believing that they could change one another and quickly realized that neither of them would give up what they wanted for the other. She wanted to have children, and he did not.

Paul and I spent our evenings together chatting about our careers and what we desired in life. I was obviously still in a cultural turmoil regarding having children. It had become a "thing" with every man I dated; either they could not wait to have children with me, or they already had children in their lives. I remember vividly that when I explained this to Paul, he said, "Robin, just choose it."

In that moment, I heard, "Choose the life you desire." Some of you might think this is obvious, for others it might seem impossible; these are the moments that you only recognize once you have them. For the first time in my life, I was honoured and respected for my life choices. His wise words, "just choose it," echoed through me and made my body vibrate. Choose it, just choose it, choose what I would like, choose what works for me, and choose what I desire … the light went on! Choosing for me—a whole new concept that changed my world. A whole new way of seeing life opened up for me, and a new reality became available to me!

I had come to a new way of being. Realizing that this was actually a choice was the first step toward making a space for me to be okay with myself. I had connected to something inside of me. I could safely stand in my own space and not judge myself as right, wrong, inept, broken. I was just *me*. Until this point, without being cognizant of it, I had waffled in my choices, taking others' judgments to heart. Now standing in my own space, I saw those judgments as their points of view—not mine! This realization was absolutely freeing and made things clearer for me. I came home a changed person and ready for more change. Do you have a TSN® Turning Point in your life or have you not created yours yet?

I will be honest; this was just the beginning. There were still many times when inner conflict ruled and finding what I truly desired seemed scary, foreign, and far away. Learning to be in allowance of my choices and not judge myself was a brand-new concept, a tool I could use and practise. I had just connected to a muscle I did not know I had. I had to train myself to work with it and strengthen it. While uncovering this new connection to myself, I stumbled upon alternative healing. The more alternative therapy courses I took, the more I realized there was to explore. In the midst of my search, I discovered a freedom that I had not yet known. A freedom that allowed me to create more of who I am. Do you have freedom in creating who you are?

The Circle Theory

In one of the courses I took, I was introduced to the circle theory, and my whole reality changed.. I learned to choose action instead of reaction to every point of view coming at me. Do you choose to live your life in action? Or do you limit yourself by only reacting? The circle helped me realize how much of our lives are based in judgment without us being cognitively aware of it. I had to share this realization with the world. This was the start of creating this book.

The circle theory explains what judgment is, how judgments can trap you, and how judgments influence what you choose for your life. Judgments control us, creating conflict and the polarity of concepts such as right and wrong, good and bad, etc. in our minds and thus in our lives. The circle visualization is about stepping back and noticing the polarity but choosing beyond it. The center of the circle represents peace and balance, and the circumference of the circle represents other peoples' *interesting points of view* as well as all the different energies that are accessible to us at any given time.

Take a moment to picture one hundred people standing in a circle. You are standing in the center, not moving. The one hundred people look at you from the edge of the circle. Each person has a different perspective, a different view of you. The person directly in front of you sees that you have two eyes, a nose, a chin, a chest, hips, thighs, knees, and toes. The person right behind you sees the back of your head, your neck, back, butt, calves, and heels. Now, because you are not moving, the person behind you does not know the colour of your eyes, and the person in front of you may not know how long your hair is. Some would agree you have two hands, two feet, and so on. Each person can describe a bit of you, but you know in your heart that you are more than what any one person can describe. Their descriptions from their respective vantage points reflect their interesting points of view of you. You are more than the total of what those one hundred people can describe, and you are more than what you can describe. Any individual description provides just an interesting point of view. Any of those interesting points of view is another energy that you can choose to embody at any time.

Imagine standing in the middle of the circle – and everyone having just an interesting point of view of you. No one is right and no one is wrong and you are just you!

You are more than what one hundred people can describe from the edges of the circle. You are more than any words that try to define you. You are more than what you can perceive. Words limit the description of you. Are you willing to be you without any definition?

If someone dropped into the middle of the circle an alien you have never seen before, and then removed it, in trying to re-create what you saw you would want to talk to all one hundred of those people to get a full description and each of their opinions would be worth just one per cent of the overall perspective. This would be the same with either the alien or you inside the circle. So, a judgment from any one is worth just one per cent of you.

Psychologists disagree on just how many personality traits there might be, and the number varies dramatically from one expert to the next. Gordon Allport, a Harvard Ph.D., suggested there were more than four thousand different personality traits to observe in a person. So, when someone says something about you, it describes just one of possibly four thousand identifiable human traits. This equates to much less than one per cent of an opinion of you. Let that sink in!

How much importance do you place on someone's opinion of you? Often it feels like much more than one per cent. If someone says, "As a woman, you need to bear children; that is what you are supposed to do," that is their perspective, their interesting point of view. If you take it to heart like I did, you are buying it as true. And it is less than one per cent of a description of you from someone else. Based on someone's one percent perspective I could not consider myself a good woman because I was unwilling to bear children and I let this judgment get to me until I understood that it was simply just an interesting point of view. The funny thing is we often let that interesting point of view rule our decision-making. It really puts people's points of view into perspective, does it not? Remember this the next time someone has an opinion of you. Do you give someone's opinion of you more than one per cent of your thoughts? Ask yourself how much you are giving them and remind yourself that it is just one interesting point of view.

Let us go back to you standing in the center of the circle. Imagine the circle as a large disc perfectly balanced with you standing in the very center of a circle, equidistant to each point on the circumference, not giving more weight to anyone "side" (or point of view) of the circle. Inner peace is disrupted when someone says something that you react to and you leave the center of the circle, tipping the balance. When you leave the center, you have made someone else's opinion of you more significant than the other perspectives, and more significant than maintaining balance in the center, which is YOU.

When someone says, "You are so pretty," we tend to gravitate toward them, leaving the center of the circle, because that comment makes us feel good. It is a positive judgment; how could it lead us astray? Is it not lovely when someone thinks we are pretty or smart or sexy or brilliant? This is their interesting point of view. It is still less than one per cent of the four thousand possible characteristics and perspectives about us. When someone says something positive to us, we like to gravitate toward that so we do not have to look at what we really think of ourselves; we can just believe what they think or say and live by their point of view. Not looking at ourselves and what we see is a way of creating a disconnection with ourselves, leading to not knowing our strength, our potency.

But do you really want to live by what someone else thinks of you, positive or negative? Or would you rather be yourself, whoever that is in any given moment? Putting yourself in the center of the circle gives you the freedom of total choice. Being you, with no point of view, is stepping into the strength of you. This is the art of choosing you: choosing to go beyond judgment, whether it is positive or negative.

When you leave the center of the circle to be with the one who says, "You are pretty," you are allowing others to control you. When you make what they say significant, you have to subtract parts of you so that you line up with what they see and think. You are not standing in the center of the circle but on their side of it, clinging to the edge, allowing their view to dictate what you see of yourself, and what you allow others to see as well. If others are only ever allowed to see you as pretty you will forever be clinging to that edge of the circle and this restricts you. At the center of the circle, you can see everything, you have more choice and the horizon is endless. If you only identify with being "pretty," then every time you are judged as "not pretty," you must tip the disc further to prove you are pretty, further restricting what is possible for you.

In this world, the opposite of almost everything exists. The opposite opinion of "You are pretty" can exist as "You are ugly." If someone calls you "ugly," you can resist them, saying, "No I am not! I am pretty because the other person says I am pretty." You are now jumping back and forth to either defend and react to a point of view or agree and align with another point of view. You are choosing to live in reaction to what others are saying to you.

How much energy is that taking up? Would it be easier, and take less energy to stand in the center and allow both opinions to just move through you like the wind through the branches of a tree? You are still rooted in who you are and what you know, never allowing anything to push you over. Either point of view can uproot you if you feed it. You may be thinking that "You are pretty" is a positive point of view; what is wrong with keeping that going? When you live by the perspective of "I am so pretty," you judge yourself every time you are not "pretty"—every time you wake up with bedhead or get caught in a rainstorm. I remember being at the gym and overhearing one lady comment to her friend as they were working out, how much she would love to be able to wear shorts while she worked out, but she could not because of how she feared people would judge the way she looked. She was sacrificing her own comfort to align with the point of view that her legs were not pretty enough for shorts!

Every judgment, good or bad, keeps you from truly seeing all of you and what is possible in your life. Every judgment, positive or negative, takes you out of the strength of being all of you, and being all of you is what living in the center of the circle means. There is joy and balance in being all of you and not allowing other points of view of you to create your view of yourself. Do you see all of you, or do you only see yourself through the projections of others?

You are more than what one person can describe. You are more than what you can describe. For at any moment in time, we are beautiful to some people and ugly to others. Some may see me as overweight and judge that. Others may wish to be the weight I am and idolize it. People are looking at you from their point of view, which is more about them than it is about you because they are looking at you through all of their own filters. Their filters are not for you to change, it is up to them to change their own filters, in their own time. Are you able to look at yourself with no filters?

Are you able to stand in the center of the circle and realize that everyone has just an interesting point of view of you? They do not define you; you get to choose who or what you become at any given moment. Who you are, and who are you willing to be is up to you. You can choose something different at any moment. You can embody any one of those interesting points of view to get the task completed from one moment to the next.

When people around you judge you, or when you judge yourself, please use this tool: Visualize yourself as a tree, rooted in all of you; all judgements, whether positive or negative, are the wind. The tree neither resists nor follows the wind, it stays rooted and grounded where it is with no point of view and nothing to prove, in total allowance of the wind flowing through its leaves and branches. Breathe into that energy and allow all judgements to flow through you just like the wind flows through the leaves. Stay rooted in who you are. Be you as the judgments flow right through you. Do not resist and do not go with the flow of the judgments. Allow yourself to let go of points of views or judgments that no longer serve you. Just like leaves fall in the season of autumn, allow old beliefs, old limitations and judgments to fall away; allow yourself to let them go just as the tree does not try to hang on to the leaves that it no longer needs.

When you are like a tree, rooted in who you are, judgment flows right through your leaves like the wind; it does not have to uproot you. Be you and allow the judgments to flow right through you.

The wind reflects different perspectives on our lives at any given time and can change at any given moment. A tree allows its leaves and branches to sway with the wind, but always remains rooted at its centre. Do you allow your views of you and your life to change? Are you holding onto old points of view that are holding you back from being more? Years ago, when I became a firefighter, I, along with others, believed I did it to prove women could do the job. However, many years later I realized I picked a career where I believed fewer people would judge me for not having children. This characteristic of mine was hidden from even me. Would I have made a different choice if I had been more conscious of this at the time? Maybe, maybe not. I do not judge it, though, as it was a choice I made in that moment. Are you willing to let go of the judgments you have of yourself for past choices? Are you able to embrace each interesting past choice, knowing you now have a new choice? Are you willing to create yourself and your life beyond judgments? Are you willing to be the tree and be you without definition?

Just as a tree lets go of its' leaves in the fall, you can let go of any limiting points of views that no longer server you. What judgments of you or others could you let go of today?

Polarity: Creating Limitations in Your Life

The circumference of the circle is made up of all possible perspectives of you; it also represents all possible energies—ones we would label as both positive and negative, and the goal in life is to be able to look at all of them without judgment. We, however, go into the polarity of seeing the negative half as "bad" and the positive half as "good."

We were trained to have our head brain rather than our heart brain run our reality. Our brains are constantly trying to decide which perspective belongs on the positive side and which belongs on the negative side. This creates polarity in everything we are, say, or do. The polarity is exhibited when we are deciding things like what is right or wrong, good or bad, safe or hazardous. This polarity disrupts the energies around us, which, ideally, are flowing freely all around us. More on energies in the chapter; Introduction to energy. This polarity keeps us in our head and out of our heart. It is with our heart that we feel the joy in our lives.

We are influenced by the expectations of our families, our communities and society. Many of us choose to not "rock the boat" and that choice may be conscious or unconscious. We create an addiction to right and wrong, good and bad, in order to avoid being judged; meanwhile, this addiction creates its own judgment of everything in our lives. There are some people who are trying to stay positive in their lives, but my sense is that they are still in constant judgment of everything. Often, there are situations that can seem quite negative at first and the need to stay positive all the time may not allow them to see the potential. It is the judgment that constricts the free flow of energy and restricts their lives without them even knowing it. The following is a little story to demonstrate what I mean:

There is a Taoist story of an old farmer who had worked his crops for many years. One day his horse ran away. Upon hearing the news, his neighbours came to visit. "Such bad luck," they said sympathetically.

"Maybe, maybe not" the farmer replied. The next morning the horse returned, bringing with it three other wild horses. "How wonderful!" the neighbours exclaimed.

"Maybe, maybe not" replied the old man. The following day, his son tried to ride one of the untamed horses, was thrown, and broke his leg. The neighbours again came to offer their sympathy for his misfortune, "Such bad luck," they said.

"Maybe, maybe not" answered the farmer. The day after, military officials came to the village to draft young men into the army. Seeing that the son's leg was broken, they passed him by. The neighbours congratulated the farmer on how well things had turned out, "Oh, how lucky that your son was not drafted," they told him.

"Maybe, maybe not" said the farmer.

In this story, we see how the farmer chooses to remain in allowance of every circumstance; he is living in the center of the circle. He does not align and agree nor resist and react to the judgments and opinions of his neighbours. Instead, he allows all the energies to contribute to what is being created in his life. How many times have you bought or believed other people's judgments and opinions and made them your own, only to create stress and upset in your life? How much easier could your life be if you simply chose not to buy the stories or others' interesting points of view of you? It is this ability to choose allowance for yourself and others that allow you to create your life beyond judgment and choose more of you.

I remember teaching the circle theory to some lovely students. Someone said to me, "Robin, so killing is just a point of view?"

"Exactly," I replied.

The student was dazed. She was at a loss for words as she tried to wrap her head around this concept that the killing energy is something one could choose.

Then I asked her, "If someone was about to hurt one of your children, what would you do?"

She said, "I would choose the killing energy to stop them."

Making yourself wrong after a situation has passed puts you right back into the polarity of the situation. The polarity of making yourself either right or wrong is what keeps you away from the strength of you. Stress is created by making someone either wrong or right about a situation. When you are stressed, you can ask: Who am I making right, and who am I making wrong? Stress is created by the polarity that we have created in our mind with judgment. When we are able to see that any perspective is possible and that any perspective can be used to create a desired outcome, we can be in allowance of the positive and negative as different energies that become tools to help us in achieving our desired outcome. By choosing the "negative" killing energy, it becomes a tool to save her children. Can you see how the killing energy would be useful when dealing with illness? Would you not like your body to kill the virus, bacteria, cancer cell, etc.? What if you could *kill* your limitations? If you believe the killing energy is always "bad" and you do everything to avoid it, how can you invoke it when you require it to serve you?

Polarity is defining what is right and what is wrong in your mind. It is black and white. It is good and bad. It is constantly fighting the negative because we so desperately want to believe in the positive, and it causes you to bounce back and forth from one side of the circle to the other, creating stress and imbalance. We feel that believing in the positive is how we are going to create a better life. If we are unwilling to look at something that we perceive to be negative in our lives, we lock out half of the circle of possibilities. By locking out the negative, we create barriers and limitations in our lives.

Where in your life could you lower your barriers, crush your limitations and find more possibility? Seeing the circle as a whole and not two separate halves creates more possibilities in our lives. Stepping out of judgment might be quite a novel concept to many of us—it is a whole new way of being and experiencing life. Do you desire more possibilities? Or do you enjoy letting judgment limit you?

Does Judgment Hold You Hostage?

The theory of the circle is to demonstrate that any judgment is just one perspective of any given situation—just an interesting point of view. It is not a definition to hold in place forever. Judgment is about controlling yourself or others, and it is always a limitation. Where does judgment begin? It begins in our brains our brain is designed to list the facts or known points of view about a situation. It is designed to make a "pro and con" list about everything around us. When we experience something, the brain instantly goes into filing mode, "Is this something good for me, or is it something bad for me?" and, "Which list do I put this in?" It is always on alert to judge and decipher; your brain is designed to do this. Thousands of years ago, our brain needed to differentiate between what was good and what was bad to keep us safe and alive. As cave dwellers, we would use our senses to judge whether that animal coming toward us was going to eat us or be useful to us, or whether a certain plant was safe or poisonous to eat. Nowadays, we use the same senses to judge others in attempt to know whether we can trust them or not. We are always judging ourselves to know whether we can trust ourselves. We use this judgment to create a sense of control and order based on how past experiences have turned out for us; generally we try to apply the same logic that "got us a win" in the past, and try to avoid repeating circumstances that made us feel vulnerable. This control of ourselves is what we use to try and avoid being judged, but we typically end up holding parts of ourselves hostage. We do not recognize that the same vulnerable feeling is what allow us to experience the joy of life—pain is on the opposite side of the circle from pleasure, but it is in the center where we experience the peace and joy of balance. I have noticed over the years that when people judge themselves nonstop, fighting to stay on one side of the circle or the other, they are not pleasurable to be around. They are not truly joyful or in balance and I believe we can pick up when they are judging us even though it may be silently in their head. Without being consciously aware of this, they drive people away. Are you driving people away? Are you holding your inner self hostage with particular judgments or points of view? When we hold our inner self hostage, we barricade ourselves in, we hide, and pretend, and morph against our true self in order to try and avoid "uncomfortable" situations. We judge ourselves harshly, and fight against discomfort and vulnerability, feeling that our true self is too blemished for the world to accept. Even if you feel the judgment is necessary to create something better, it is still judgment and it still limits possibilities. We create a world where we feel we are not even allowed to be ourselves. Judgment constricts the true you and what you are choosing for your life. However, by choosing to be in balance at the center of the circle, we can see ourselves and our circumstances from all points of view—even the painful or uncomfortable ones, the vulnerable ones. When we can be in balance and allowance of all points of view and all the energies around the circle, this is where empowerment lies. The inner self no longer needs to be held hostage, stuck in or clinging to one point of view or the other for fear of judgment, because everything is now just an interesting point of view. Being like the tree, strongly rooted with the wind (judgments) flowing through and around it; or like the Taoist farmer, in allowance of all of life's circumstances, is what allows us to embrace our true self and be more potent every day. When we allow ourselves to see that it is not necessary to control ourselves or others with judgment, then we can step into the potency of who we truly are without trying to prove anything to anyone. What if our raw, uncovered face is exactly what the world needs to see? If we can be vulnerable and real with ourselves first and own it, we can invite others to do the same. Then, we become untouchable by judgment. The less people judge themselves, the less likely they are to judge others and the more fun they are to be around.

If you have ever been lucky enough to be around a person who did not judge themselves or you, you probably noticed how liberating it felt. It is intoxicating to be with such a person, and you can lower all your barriers and just be yourself, with no point of view. Knowing every judgment is just an interesting point of view lets us orchestrate what we desire to create in our lives instead of living in reaction to what others say. I often hear celebrities and other successful people, when interviewed, say things like "Everyone called me nuts for doing it, but I chose it anyway." They were aware of others judging them. However, they chose to go beyond the judgment to create whatever it was they desired. When you step out of judgment and the need to feel in control, you become someone that others desire to be around. You become more of you.

Freedom is being you in any situation despite any judgments or points of view delivered at you. Are you willing to choose this freedom for you?

When you can hear a "negative judgment" about yourself and be in allowance of it, rather than react to it, you can choose beyond it and take action toward what you truly desire to create in your life. If someone says to me, "You are ugly," I can perceive that there are times in my life I am ugly, or times when I am willing to get "ugly"—fighting fires is a messy business, after all. Or, if somebody says to me, "you are such a bitch!" I am thinking, that is right! And that is exactly who you want putting out the fire when your house is burning!" You see, either of those comments are just different perspectives of me in any moment, and I know there have been times when I have chosen to embody the energy of whatever they are judging on me. Similarly, when someone says, "You are so smart," I can perceive there are times in my life when I am smart and there are times when I am not. Judgments that are meant to be compliments can also trip us up if we align and agree with them— "Wow! You are Supermom"! If you align with that, you may also react by putting extra pressure on yourself to always live up to that judgment. There are times we have been smart and there are times we have been ugly. You can step into allowance of someone's judgment of you by saying to them, or even just thinking, "Wow—interesting perspective. What else do you think?" This is allowing the energy of what was said to go right through your body and your being, without aligning, agreeing, resisting or reacting to it. It is our reaction and resistance or our aligning and agreeing to something that creates angst in us. This angst creates tension in our body, and thus we are not bendable like a tree and may crack under pressure. Judgment can only hurt us if we align and agree with it or resist and react to it. Recognizing judgment as just an interesting point of view is a great tool that can give you more space and freedom to be all of you. What would your life be like if you were to stop judging yourself? Can you perceive how much more open your life could be? Not judging yourself for the choices you make allows you to choose to embody whatever energy or point of view that works for you in any given moment. By choosing not to judge yourself, you also invite others to not judge you, nor themselves, and that creates freedom! Are you willing to have the freedom of no judgment of you?

Allowance: Expanding the Possibility of You and Your Life

Allowance is the ability to be all of you, without limitations, judgments or definitions. To perform a task or achieve a goal may require you to choose a certain way of being, a certain energy. You then allow yourself to step out of the center of the circle and be a certain way. After the task is complete or the goal is reached, you allow yourself to return to the center of the circle. Allowance is coming back to the center and not judging what you have just chosen to be in that prior moment. When you choose to be yourself and inhabit the center of the circle, in addition to joy and balance in your life, you are choosing your strength and potency. When you choose what you believe others desire of you and go against yourself, you choose against your potency. We *can* be all energies (ways of being), we simply choose what is required in the moment.

Living in allowance of judgment does not mean you become a doormat and allow others to walk all over you; that may require boundaries and the aggressive or assertive energy to enforce them. Being in allowance is not about allowing others to belittle you; it is about 'not' allowing yourself to be controlled by your reactions to others and their judgments and/or interesting points of views. It is being yourself without needing to prove it to anyone.

Allowance means not allowing yourself to be controlled by the polarity of any situation or circumstance. It means not feeling guilty or regretting whatever side of the circle you choose in any given moment. Allowance means being yourself regardless of whether others are resisting and reacting to you or agreeing and aligning with you. Allowance is being free of judgment of all points of view from everyone, including yourself.

Every perspective around the circle is just a choice of who you are at that moment and does not define who you are all the time. The point bears repeating, with emphasis: every perspective around the circle is just a choice of the energy you can embody at *that moment* and *does not* define who you are all the time. Some moments in life may require you to be aggressive. As a firefighter I would choose to be aggressive to extinguish the fire. I embody the energy of aggression for that moment to get the job done, and then go back to the center of the circle, let the aggressiveness go, and ask myself, "What other energy can I be now?"

The trick to letting things go is to not judge yourself when you were aggressive by thinking you were wrong to choose that energy—I do not go home later and worry that I came across as too aggressive when I was putting out the fire. When I spend a day teaching in a beautiful dress and I get a flat tire on the way home, I can choose to embody a more vulnerable energy and ask someone for help to change my tire. Could I have changed it myself? Of course! But I choose something different in that moment—to keep my pretty dress clean and enjoy the receiving energy of watching a capable, possibly even sexy, man work on my truck! The key here is that I did not make myself wrong for not changing my own tire. I am fully capable of doing it, and on any other day I might have, but I am not wrong to choose to ask for help. True allowance is knowing you can choose what will work for you in any moment. I choose to embody whatever energy I require, from any perspective of the circle to achieve what I desire in any moment. I still remain rooted in the center of the circle and do not allow opinions or judgments define who or what I am. I do not allow them to make me wrong for choosing a certain energy. When you choose to embody a particular energy to get the job done and then judge it as wrong, you are choosing against who you are because who you are is made up of all the energies; when you judge any of them, you limit who you can be in that moment. Such judgments constrict you and in turn restrict what is possible in your life. When you ask the question, "Who am I?" whatever energy on the edge of the circle you choose defines you for only that moment. Are you willing to be any energy that is available? Do you feel that? This is an enormous question. Are you willing to be any energy or to see yourself from any perspective in order to expand your life into something greater? Even though I chose not to become a mother, I can choose that energy to care for my co-workers and create a happier workplace. I did not make the mother energy wrong, nor did I choose to live my life as a mother. It is just an energy I can choose if the situation requires a mother.

How many of us have created ourselves by what others tell us we are? We buy it, believing it to be true all the time, and we create that point of view within ourselves. If people tell you that you are a good listener and you buy into that, you may look for ways to be a good listener and create your life, and maybe even your career, around that. Please know that you can choose to embody any type of energy imaginable at any given moment. In that moment you were a good listener, this does not mean you have to be a good listener all the time. There are times that being a good listener will serve us and there are times when not being a good listener will serve us.

If there are perspectives or energies on the edge of the circle that you can not imagine choosing, there is a break in the flow of energy around the circle. When you are unwilling to embody, or even acknowledge, any one of the energies, that becomes the energy that controls you. Where is the freedom in that? If you are unwilling to embody the killing energy then you are unwilling to kill your limitations and thus stay stuck in the past. I love to embody what some might call "the bitch" energy when it is time to take charge and put out a fire. Be willing to embody any or all of the energies—and be willing to embody any energy beyond what you are currently familiar with. Acknowledging that a certain energy is available to you is different than choosing it. You do not need to choose every energy, but you must be *willing to be* every energy to be all of you. Are you willing to choose that for your life and living?

Knowing that you can choose anything is true empowerment; it is knowing you have your own back and will be there for yourself. It means anyone can say anything to you and it will not shake you off balance or out of the center of the circle. Being in allowance without judgment is how you create space and peace within your life, within you.

When you choose allowance for yourself, it may inspire others to choose it for themselves as well. Allowance is acknowledgement of everything as a gift, moving on and having no attachments to it. Are you willing to be the gift of you to yourself and others? Being in allowance is knowing that you, and others, can change at any moment and not drawing conclusions about who you are or who they are.

Being in allowance is when nothing or no one is more significant than you and you being balanced in the center of the circle. It is standing in the center of the circle metaphorically and wondering: What else is possible here? What can I create? Who or what can I be in this moment?

Invalidating Others' Points of View

Let us imagine that you are standing in the center of the circle and the person behind you is judging you as ugly. Have you ever wanted everyone to see how attractive you are? You could force that person to move to the side of the circle that sees you as attractive. You are basically telling them or showing them how to think, and I believe no one likes to be told what to think or do. They are standing on the edge of the circle and all they can see is your ugliness. The more you try to pull them over to the other point of view, the uglier you become to them. Allowing people—whether they are family, your best friend, a work colleague, or even a stranger—to see you as *they* see you is true empowerment, for both them and you. Do you allow others to have their points of view of you? Even negative ones? Have you that much strength? Or do you let their points of view take you away from your potency? How potent would you be if you did not allow other's points of view of you to create a reaction in you?

I did a presentation on the theory of the circle, and I described the polarity of being smart or stupid. "Please remember," I said, "that there have been times in most of our lives when we have been smart and times when we have been stupid. Being willing to learn from either is how we expand who we are."

A woman approached me after the presentation to make me wrong for using the word "stupid." She was adamant that she was correct to never use it. To appease her, I said essentially, "You are correct; next time I will use 'not smart' in my presentation." I could tell I was not going to change her mind in that moment. I was invalidating her reality by using the word "stupid" to describe someone. She had even told her children and grandchildren that they were never allowed to use this word. In her eyes, I was wrong for using the word in my presentation, and she was right. I have no opinion about being wrong in her eyes for using the word "stupid." However, if I were to make myself wrong for using the word "stupid," then that word would control me, and I would lose my freedom to choose what I desire to say. I had inadvertently invalidated how she had chosen to live her life, which was by never using the word "stupid." Do you think never allowing herself to use the word constricts her world or expands it? In my world, not being able to use a word to describe the energy of something for fear I may upset another would be restrictive. How many of us have constricted ourselves so we do not offend or upset others?

Does refusing to use certain words or the energy of the word give this woman freedom, or does it limit her possibilities? Not only does she take away her own freedom by not using the word; it locks her into judgment and restricts her possibilities when someone else uses the word "stupid." She created a lot of defence around this word and she demanded that all around her had to live life her way. Is that creating freedom for her or them?

Let us look at the word "stupid." It means to lack meaning, sense and/or understanding. The opposite word of "stupid" could be "smart." There have been times in my life when I was smart, and times I have been stupid; both were learning times for me. I would not like to limit my learning times in life; would you? Another way of looking at the word "stupid" could bring this thought: "What a wonderful way to be open to learning more in life." If someone believes they are smart, they might be closed to learning from others, because they believe they already know everything. Being open to experiencing "stupid" would be a great way to learn and grow, to be more of you, and to know what is possible. By looking at another perspective of the word "stupid" opens a different possibility for that word, and then the word does not control you. In some countries, it has been less than a hundred years since women gained the right to vote. The idea that women would want to vote, obviously seemed stupid to some people, or they would not have restricted it in the first place. The women's suffragists invalidated this point of view by demanding the vote. And by the same token, it probably seemed stupid (senseless) to the suffragists that they were not allowed to vote. What if they had just aligned and agreed with the idea that it was ridiculous for women to vote? Perhaps, the situation would have stayed the same. In having our own points of view, it is inevitable that we will invalidate someone else's point of view. Either side could argue why they are right (or why the other is wrong) until the cows come home, the only thing making it so is that there are opposing points of view in the first place. In order for change and progress to have happened, somewhere someone had to be open to the energy of new possibilities. Do you allow yourself to be any energy in any moment to have freedom of being yourself and looking at what else is possible? Being yourself will inevitably clash with what someone else thinks is right or wrong, are you willing to be yourself anyway?

Were there times in your life when others invalidated your point of view and you tried to make them wrong? To see that there are many points of view on any issue, or any word, creates true empowerment for all. It creates more freedom for all of us to choose what works for us.

Others could not relate to my reality of not wanting children or marriage. Instead of saying, "Cool choice, Robin," they listed all the reasons why I was wrong for choosing this. It was their interesting point of view of life, their judgment of their own lives, and they were imposing it on everyone around them, including me. If we had all been in allowance of one another's points of view, there would have been a lot less inner conflict and conflict for all of us.

My reality of no kids and no marriage seemed to invalidate what they had chosen, so they tried to make me wrong for my choices. People who judged me wanted me to get married and have kids to validate the fact that they had chosen that for themselves. When others choose what you choose, it may seem to validate your choices. But if you are judging others, it is because you feel that their choices are invalidating your own. If you are doing what you truly desire, there is no need to prove to anyone that what you are doing is right or wrong or good or bad, it just is. What I am saying here is that you can use that energy of judgment to learn more about yourself and your choices. You can ask yourself, "What am I feeling here? Why do I feel I need to convince them?" or "Why do I feel that their choice is wrong, or that my choice is better than theirs?" As we examine what is beneath our judgment, we also let go of our need for it and we are able to see other perspectives. We are able to see all perspectives with more clarity.

If someone invalidates your reality, does that make you look at your reality and see how you have created it? I could have gone into the wrongness of using the word, or acknowledging the energy of, "stupid" and made myself feel bad that I had really upset someone with it. At that moment when the woman disagreed with me, I lowered my energetic barriers and totally received what she said. I knew there was a learning moment for me here in seeking allowance to have no point of view on either side. As I was not able to see all aspects of using the word "stupid", I knew I needed to consult with someone to assist me in seeing all aspects of the word "stupid". An amazing friend, Julia, helped me to understand that I had invalidated this lady's strong belief. Then I was able to see it as a moment of growth for myself and make neither her, nor myself, wrong for our interesting points of view of the word "stupid."

If people choose something for their lives and it does not go against what others have chosen, there is no invalidation of a reality; their choice actually seems to validate the reality they have created around them. My point of view of "stupid" invalidated her reality, and she fought back—which was fine. By me choosing allowance, I did not have to go into reaction and feed her fight.

Let us look at being a vegetarian. People that choose to be vegetarian have researched and chosen it because they believe it is best for them and their bodies. When others around them question their choice, it may be that they are really questioning their own nutritional choices and this causes them to resist and react to the vegetarian's choice—they are trying to make being a vegetarian wrong to prove, or feel better about their own choice to consume meat. I believe that, deep down, they are unsure about nutrition and question their own choices. This can go the other way, with vegetarians trying to make those who choose to eat meat wrong.

When someone challenges our beliefs or decisions, a lot of us feel this is an invalidation of our personal choices. When we are not in total allowance, every point of view that is different from ours will invalidate our own. Feeling invalidated puts up our energetic barriers and takes us away from the center of the circle. When you feel invalidated, could it be because you are making your point of view about something significant? When you start looking for validation of every point of view you have, you bring polarity into your life. This polarity creates a roller coaster of emotions urging you to judge against or for a particular point of view. A point of view is only good for the moment in which you require it. So, whether you are a meat-eater or vegetarian or vegan, peacefulness can be created if everyone is able to choose total allowance of this.

We judge others to fit them into a box because we think we can control what they will or will not do; to decide who we think they should be. We judge ourselves, and others judge us, and we use these judgments to create and define who we think we should be. Are you willing to let go of judgment to create more choice and possibilities in your life? Are you willing to step outside the box of judgment? Are you willing to be yourself even if it may invalidate others' views of the world?

The Center of the Circle – Do you have an Agenda?

You can be in the center of the circle and allow yourself to be seen from every angle. Likewise, we can put any issue in the center of the circle and realize it also can be seen from every angle. What issue could you examine at the center of the circle to gather more awareness about it?

Anything can be put in the center of the circle, symbolically; when you put it there, it allows you the space to see it from every possible perspective. Putting a relationship in the center of the circle, you are invited to see every aspect of that relationship. Once you can see every aspect, you will be able see if that relationship will contribute to your life or not. You can do this with anything: a job, God, religion, and even your spouse. Putting your spouse in the center of the circle, seeing them completely, and being in allowance of them is true caring; it is true empowerment for them and for you. Most people in the beginning of a relationship will typically put the other person in the center of the circle and view them only from the positive half of the circle. Doing this, we can pretend that person is perfect for us. If we do not walk around the entire circumference of the circle to see them fully, we set ourselves up for disappointment later in the relationship. Are you willing to see every aspect of you, your spouse, or any other relationship you have created?

When we have an agenda, as in, we are looking for a certain aspect in someone or a particular topic, we tend to stand on that side of the circle and therefore see it again and again. You may be looking for evidence that your spouse dismisses your love to prove you should end the relationship. You will unconsciously be watching them from that angle of the circle and therefore be keenly aware anytime they dismiss your love. You are limiting your view of their actions. You are looking at them through a filter, creating what you think you should see. Ideally, by putting them in the center of the circle and being able to walk around the entire circumference with no agenda, no attachment, and no expectations, you are able to see times when they dismiss your love and times when they honour it. Having the ability to see them from all sides, whether honouring or dismissive, allows you to not be offended by what they do or say, now or in the future. When you view someone or something with an agenda, you are no longer allowing the flow of energy around the circle or seeing all perspectives, but are rather stuck in one perspective, projecting into the centre from that viewpoint; you are looking at the issue through that lens only. You are projecting what you expect to see and ignoring other possibilities. It limits how we can see this person or issue and creates judgment instead. It begs the question, "See?" I knew it! I knew they did not appreciate my love. I should end this relationship! How can I stay with someone who does not appreciate me?" You only see this outcome because of your agenda and limited view of the circle.

Do you use agendas or project onto others to prove your judgments are true? Does this create freedom for them or for you?

This is how you allow yourself to live without polarity and with total allowance for yourself and everyone around you. It is an art to choose you and to choose beyond judgment. If you come with preconceived notions of what a relationship should or should not be, then you are coming to a relationship with an incomplete circle of possibilities and setting up the relationship for possible failure. If you are coming into a relationship expecting it to fulfill certain expectations, you are coming to the relationship with certain agendas and therefore limiting what it could be. If you believe a relationship will complete you and make you whole, every time you do not feel whole you have to make the other person wrong. Making them wrong creates limitations in your relationship. Being open to possibilities and not drawn to conclusions of how the other should be or act in a relationship keeps that relationship open to more possibilities. Being able to see yourself as whole before entering a relationship is empowering. How many people choose a relationship to define themselves?

The circle theory can illuminate any circumstance. If you put a certain date in the middle, this allows you to see it fully. When you make what happened on a certain date significant, you may be controlled by that date. The other day, my partner, Gary, had his 65th birthday, and we had an enjoyable morning sleeping in together. For us being able to be with each other in the morning is rare with our full schedules. In the afternoon, he was busy making apple pie (his favourite), and I was going out for a walk with a friend of mine. My friend seemed upset to discover it was Gary's birthday and we had nothing special planned. She made me wrong for not making Gary's birthday special; in her mind, she felt sorry for Gary. Gary and I celebrate our lives together, and the contribution we are to each other, many times throughout the year. This does not need to be confined to a specific day. We do not have many days where we are able to take it slow and enjoy each other's company, so on this day we enjoyed doing special activities together. If we had made his birthday significant, we would have judged ourselves and each other for either doing it right or doing it wrong. Putting a day in the center of a circle and not being tied to one aspect of it allows you to have choices of what you desire to create in any given moment. If you make something significant, it controls you and gives you no choice but to make you wrong or others wrong when it is not fulfilled. This, again, is judgment, notice the many ways judgment is used by you or others and the restriction it creates in one's life.

Play with the theory of the circle. Put many different people, events, or situations in the center and allow yourself to see all their different aspects. This knowledge of the circle created so much freedom for me. Even for meetings at work, I am able to see how others can look at a situation from a totally different angle. It frees me from making myself wrong for my perspective and it frees them from me making them right or wrong. It is incredible how much my life has changed since I have embraced the tool of the circle. What could you change in your life that would allow you to go beyond judgment and go for what you truly desire to create in your life?

The Illusion of Positivity

To see something as positive, one requires judgment, and I believe it is the energy of judgment that limits our lives. As soon as we judge something as positive or negative, we have gone into the polarity of the situation. We are then unable to see the situation with clarity, but rather through our filter of positive or negative. This filter is our addiction to polarity. Living in allowance of what is and being able to create your life with no judgment is how we grow. Some would say having children is positive, and for others not having children is positive. Do you see how this is still judgment? I see it as a choice, with no judgment of positive or negative. There are many aspects of having (or not having) children; all aspects require judgment to be identified as positive or negative. The myth of positivity is that "thinking positive" or just "looking on the bright side" still requires judgment and only seeing from one side of the circle, and thus creating limitation in one's life. People say, "I do not like judgmental people, they bring too much negativity into my life." These people are judging others to justify their choice of "positivity at all costs." This justification energy is a proving energy; to whom are they trying to prove something? Is "positivity" the only way to live life?

If one can choose total allowance, one can stand in the middle of the circle in their potency of who they are, with negativity all around them, and it does not sway them. This is where I desire to be. Where do you desire to be in life? Freedom is you being you, whether there is something positive or negative around you. Are you willing to choose the strength of you and be all of you?

The illusion of positivity creates an anxiety of always having to judge something as positive or negative in your life. By standing in the center of the circle, in the strength of you, you can choose allowance to create a life beyond judgment.

Empowerment of Perspective

Being in allowance means not giving anyone's perspective a controlling factor in your life. When nothing is more significant than anything else in your life, you are suddenly able to see everything as another possibility. My relationship is important to me, but it is not a controlling factor. I am able to choose what I desire in my life, and my relationship with Gary will contribute to it or not. My relationship neither defines me nor what I choose. Putting my relationship in the center of the circle allows me the freedom to see it as a choice and not something I am stuck with. I can allow it to contribute to my decisions and my choices just as any other factor.

We tend to put an issue or problem in the center of the circle, only to look at it from one perspective and then try to create our life with that one-sided point of view. The possibilities open for us when we are willing to walk around the circle and see the issue from other vantage points. When we go through a relationship breakup or divorce, we may get stuck on the question, "How could they do this to me?" We may dwell on the trauma and drama of how negatively the breakup affected our lives. What if we were able to see this breakup as an opportunity to create something greater than what existed before? There are so many aspects of a breakup, both positive and negative. Looking from all angles shows one what a gift a divorce can be. A divorce allows a person to step into their own strength and create a life from their own desires rather than the desires of others. Every breakup that I have gone through has contributed to every aspect of my life. They have allowed me to see what I desire and do not desire in a relationship, and they all contributed to me learning more about myself. I have allowed myself to step beyond the judgment, beyond any trauma and drama and see them as contributions. This has created such freedom in my life. Are you willing to choose more freedom in your life?

I have an amazing partner who honours my choices. I do my best to honour his choices too. He chooses not to share his money with me, which really bothered me for many years. One day, after putting this issue in the center of the circle, I let go of the attachments I had to all my beliefs about how a man should share his money. Rather than making him wrong, I was able to see how my partner not sharing his money with me had led me to create more in my life. It was a gift. If Gary had supported me financially, then I would not be working so hard at my job, or as a teacher and facilitator, or at writing this book. Sometimes you do not see the contribution of those in your life until you step out of the point of view you are holding onto and see it from another place around the circle. Being willing to put anything in the center of the circle, walk around it, and see the different perspectives is true empowerment. Whatever the issue is, once you see it as a contribution to your life, it no longer controls you. What are you holding onto that you are still reacting to? Are you willing to look at other perspectives and see how it has been a contribution to your life?

Not only can the circle be used to describe different perspectives of you, but when you put issues or problems inside it, you can see all the possibilities that could contribute to your growth. How could you use the circle to create more in your life?

When Judgement Triggers you

Most of us are not taught how to become our real selves due to an infinite loop of limiting judgments. When we react to something happening in our lives and it creates an emotional response of anger, fear, worry, shame or guilt, I call this an emotional charge. We all have emotional charges that require releasing from our psychology. We have all had moments and experiences that have caused us pain and often times we do not totally resolve or deal with that pain. When we do not, this memory lingers below the surface of our psyche and is triggered when a button is pushed in our lives, usually by another. The emotional pain button is there to remind us that this is a moment of growth – that we have an aspect of ourselves that is not healed and thus requires attention. The emotional charge is created by us and the button is only there due to the issue in our past that is unresolved. When a certain button is pushed, it is an opportunity to look at the emotional charge and release the old hurt by becoming aware of how it was created. If you buy a new purse, bring it home and show it to your spouse. Your spouse reacts by saying something like, "Why do you spend your money on such frivolous things? You are so irresponsible." You then feel bad and wonder if you even still want the purse; your spouse may have pushed your "self-worth button" which triggers you to justify why you deserve this purchase instead of looking at what actually triggered you in the first place: feeling that your self-worth was at risk. The emotional charge within you sends you into reaction mode instead of into the action mode of healing and resolving the underlying trigger. Are you willing to look at the button, in this case, self-worth, and discover it is more about your sense of worth? Maybe when you were younger you were made wrong for wanting more in your life. Or maybe someone told you that you were bad and did not deserve 'Santa' to bring you presents. These are over-simplifications, but whatever the case may be, these reactions will be as unique as you are, so it helps to get an unbiased trained practitioner to work at what the trigger is really all about. Once you are able to look at an event without an emotional charge, the event no longer controls you. Exploring an event without an emotional charge does not mean ignoring it; rather, it is the outcome of having learned from the issue and experiencing emotional growth. When someone negatively or positively judges you as being or doing something and it triggers you into some form of emotional reaction, recognize it as an opportunity for growth. When you hear a judgment, it is a trigger only if you have judged yourself that way before and made yourself wrong for it. If you are judged as "stupid" and it causes a reaction in you, it is only because you have judged yourself as "stupid" and made yourself wrong for being "stupid" at some point. Until you let the emotional charge go, that energy will be in your world, defining what you will or will not allow yourself to be, and it will be a trigger for you every time a judgment like that comes at you. If you can perceive the times in your life when you were "stupid" as moments of learning and growth and receive them as a gift, then being called "stupid" can no longer control you. A tool you can use when you feel judged is to say to yourself, "For every time I have been [*insert judgment*] or judged myself for being [*insert judgment*], I now let it go." Allow this energy of past judgment to dissipate and release with ease from your body and being.

Why is it so hard to give up the habit of judgment? We have been taught from a young age that it will keep us safe and help us fit in. Giving up judgment is one of the hardest things to do but giving it up is what gives you potency. These emotional charges are created from past hurts, and we hold onto to them as a way of protecting ourselves from the same hurts happening again, however we end up limiting what else we can receive in the process. Allowing yourself to release the emotional charge allows you to be more authentically you and opens you to receiving the gift in every situation.

This may be an opportunity to familiarize yourself with different modalities and their tools. One of the modalities I love is Access Consciousness. Its practitioners use a clearing statement to let go of charged emotions around a topic. The tools can instantly create a space to release the emotional charge around a judgment. It allows one to be in the moment and create clarity around a situation, like seeing "stupid" as a moment for growth and more awareness in your life. This is how you can choose allowance and have gratitude for yourself and events in your life. An emotional charge is what fuels these reactions to a judgment. Let them go by imagining yourself in the center of the circle and being in allowance.

There are many alternative healing modalities available that will allow you to release emotional charges from past situations, (for a list of suggestions and their brief descriptions see Appendix B). Important things to consider when choosing someone to help you facilitate these emotional releases are to look for someone who is trained/certified with some experience so they can guide you to go deeper as to why an emotional charge exists for you. Be open-minded and willing to receive help from others.

I have also created courses around the circle theory. One of my courses involves standing in the center of the circle and receiving the different energies. Can you stand in the center of the circle and receive that you are brilliant? Receiving and becoming any energy or perspective of you is the way you can grow into being able to embody any one of these characteristics. The introductory class that I have created is called "The Art of Choosing You!" (Please visit www.robinchant.com and www.artofchoosingyou.com for more details). Other modalities that might help include the Way of the Heart (thewayoftheheart.com); Byron Katie, *The Work* (thework.com); and the BodyTalk System (bodytalksystem.com). All of these modalities have their place; whichever resonates with you the most is what will allow you to release emotional charges of judgments and it may be that different situations call for different modalities at any given time; allow yourself to be open to trying new things at different times.

This is a whole new way of being in the world, and others may not relate to you. It is when you can choose the strength of you that you get to be you without a point of view of you and with no need to prove yourself—this is the space where you create the life you have always known you desire. It takes time and finesse to have the heart to choose you; are you willing to do that? Are you willing to choose you?

Are you always justifying your choices in life? If you are looking for the reason to choose something or not, is it really a choice or are you choosing on what you can justify? Does this give you freedom in your choices?

The Power of a Question

A question is usually asked to obtain an answer or conclusion to a situation or problem. When the question is answered it is usually a right answer or a conclusion to a certain situation. What if we asked a question to create an opportunity to invite more possibilities into one's awareness of something? Choosing to ask a question in my life has created endless possibilities, especially once I stepped out of judgment. When looking at a problem, we tend to get tunnel vision and focus on one or two solutions. Putting a problem in the center of the circle and asking, "What else is possible here?" creates space and allows different possibilities to percolate up. If you allow yourself to dwell on a question, eventually you can see many different options, and you will notice that some of the solutions that pop up will be ones you may have never thought of before. Just by imagining your problem in the center of the circle and saying, "What else is possible here?" allows the universe to serve up any number of possibilities that your inner being may become aware of. Then, a problem is not seen as something to solve; rather, it is a way to create something greater. This is the gift of living without judgment, without polarity, and being in the energy of the question. When people told me I had to have children, I secretly said to myself, "What else is possible here?" Which led me to opportunities of travel and discovering who I was beyond a mother.

In reading this book, you have probably noticed a lot of questions; they are all about getting you to look at your life and notice if you are creating as much as you desire. I once heard Gary Douglas, the founder of Access Consciousness, say that when you can receive everything as a gift in your life, it no longer controls you, and you get to be you. Are you willing to ask, "What is the gift?" in every situation? The power of the question is to invite you to more possibilities. A good question can help you create a more expansive life than you currently have. Are you willing to sit in the energy of what else is possible or are you addicted to conclusion and having a predictable life? Are you willing to be open and be more you? Are you willing to create more in your life?

When you are willing to be in the question, this invites more possibilities into your life. Be willing to ask a question when a problem arises and not just look for the one answer or the first solution.

Introduction to Energy

Everything we perceive with our eyes is physical matter in our world. This matter is made up of elements, and those elements are made up of molecules. Molecules are made up of atoms and those atoms each contain a nucleus, with one or more electrons spinning around them. If we magnified a hydrogen atom so that its nucleus were the size of a basketball, its lone electron would be found orbiting around the nucleus about two miles away![1] Between the atom and the electron there is a space full of energy created by the electromagnetic force that attracts the electron(s) to the nucleus. In an atom, how many electrons and how fast they travel around the nucleus is based on which element it is in this world. In very basic terms, this is what makes a table a table and what makes us human beings. As one may discern, we are made up of billions and billions of atoms, and most of each atom is full of energy. Technically, each of us is an energy ball with a little bit of matter.

I know many people do not like to talk about things that they cannot taste, see, smell, or touch with their senses. However, I believe they are missing the energy aspect of what exists in our world. There are concepts that are only made up of energy, like the concept of love. Love is not something you can see, but it is something you may sense with your heart. We can sense how much we love our children, but this sensing how much one loves another is outside our five senses. Even if you do not believe in this view of energy, there are times in your life that you tap into it. There are times you know who is calling before you even pick up your phone, this is because you have tapped into this person's energy. When in a relationship, you may have been able to tune into the other person's energy and know if they are having a "good" day or a "bad" day. In fact, we tap into energy all the time without acknowledging it. Do you know that energy is the first aspect of communication that we tap into? Most of us can perceive if someone we know around us is angry, and then we look for verbal and non-verbal clues to confirm what we sense. At some level, we are aware of energy, and this is a very simple explanation to demonstrate that.

---

1 https://education.jlab.org/qa/atomicstructure_05.html

Many people like to analyze everything in their brains, but this can interfere with tapping into the energy of something. We can sometimes tune into energy before something is about to happen. The more you are in your heart, and not in your brain, the easier it is to tune into the energy of something.

This might be a good time to mention the Three Brains concept from another alternative healing modality, BodyTalk. The three brains consist of the head brain, heart brain and the gut brain. The head brain, which we refer to as our brain, is meant to process and analyze information that is coming in through one or more of our five senses. This head brain is all about creating our pros and cons lists and about keeping us safe. It is not meant to live in the question but rather to answer every question that is thrown at it. It likes answers, conclusions and definitions. It is our head brain that likes things to stay the same and does not like to live in possibilities. It is also common knowledge that the head brain consists of the right and left side; these two sides are very different. Someone we would call a left-brained individual is typically more logical and detail-oriented, while those we would call right-brained are generally seen as more creative, intuitive, artistic types. Jill Bolte Taylor has an amazing video on the brain called "Stroke of Insight", which can be found on the TED Talks app or on YouTube. Bolte Taylor is a neuroanatomist who suffered a stroke in her left brain. She does an amazing job of explaining the difference between the right and left sides of our brains, and of bringing awareness to the different aspects of each. I am mentioning all of these now so you are able to be aware of when you are in your left brain or right brain too much. Being in one side all the time will create a limitation in your life. Allow both sides of your brain to contribute to your thoughts to create a more balanced life. This is to prevent you from being too logical or too focused in one area of a problem. It invites you too look at both the logical side and the creative side to figuring out what is required in a moment to create something greater.

In addition to the head brain we also have a heart brain. The heart brain is meant to help us with *how we relate* to the information (pros/cons) gathered by the head brain. It brings 'You' into the equation. The heart brain is meant to store the wisdom gleaned from previous experiences and is what we refer to when we say things like "I know it by heart," as in, it is something you do not even have to think about, and you just *know* it. Our gut brain is meant to make the decisions, not our head brain. Our head brain actually gets overwhelmed the more we try to make it come to a decision. Our gut brain is meant to integrate the information gathered by our head brain and the wisdom from the heart brain to create a gut-based decision, an instinct. Our gut reaction is the one that we are meant to follow in life, unfortunately though, most of us are taught to follow what our head brain tell us instead. I would have chosen to have children if I followed the rationalization going on in my head for that is what society was dictating to me. My gut told me I was not meant to have children in my life.

The problem is that most of us live in our heads, (and typically mostly in one side of it!), while ignoring the wisdom of the heart and its *knowing and* ignoring our gut instincts as well.

One of the best ways to be more "in your heart" or in your "knowing" is to help balance the information that the right and left sides of your head brain is processing, and tap into the awareness from your three brains; your head, heart and guts. Meditation and mindfulness practices are very useful for bringing balance in our lives. Breathing into your heart space area and getting quiet and asking yourself; "What do I truly desire?" This is to get you out of your head and into your heart. Asking your gut area; "what would you choose now?" These are all ways to get you to focus on the areas of your body so that you can create your life more with your whole being rather than just in your brain.

Now, back to energy! Energy is not positive or negative; it is our brain that categorizes it as such. Allowing the energy of a judgment to flow through you allows you to receive it into your body and entire being. Energy is your first step in communicating; it is not the words themselves but the energy of the words or experience that you tap into. Are you willing to perceive the energy of a situation, or do you go into your mind to stop it? What would your life be like if you were to perceive the energy of something with your whole being?

When speaking about our lives, we vibrate at a certain frequency—the frequency of the words we speak. Each word has its own vibrational energy and each energy attracts more of the same energy. So, when you're on the side of the circle that could be perceived as negative and you are talking about all the negative stuff in your life with enthusiasm, you are picking up more energy that is vibrating at that same frequency and attracting it to you. The universe, like a radio transmitter, notices you tuning into this frequency and responds with more of the same corresponding events in your life. The same happens when you are on the side of the circle that could be perceived as positive and telling lots of positive stories, the universe notices you tuning in to this positive frequency and gives you more of it. The universe does not have an opinion of what is good and what is bad; it just notices the energy. When you are vibrating with a certain type of energy, you are going to create more of that energy in your life.

The reason I am bringing up energy here is because most of us tap into the energy around us more than we give ourselves credit for, and I believe this discussion of energy may help you to sense energetic barriers. Being aware of when we or others are putting up these barriers, is a great way to notice when we are not choosing allowance of what is happening for us.

Energetic Barriers

Energetic barriers are created when we sense that someone is going to say or do something to hurt us, or something that we do not like. Most of us do this subconsciously to protect ourselves.

When someone says something negative to you, and you wish to ignore it, you are resisting and reacting to it; ignoring it is not allowance. Ignoring, or pretending it does not exist, puts up your energetic barriers. Others can perceive these barriers and may try to push through to feel connected to you or to prove that they are right. A good example of this is a salesperson trying to convince you to buy something; the more you resist, the more your energetic walls go up. This is like putting fuel on the fire, and now the salesperson tries even harder to convince you to buy the product. Most of this is done unconsciously but as we tune into the energy, we are able to become more aware of what is really happening.

The proving energy also triggers energetic barriers. If I believe I was meant to not have children and I must prove it to everyone, then that would have created a proving energy. As soon as people sense a proving energy, they put up their energetic barriers. Once both sides have their energetic barriers up, they are not receiving any information–only limitation. Do you realize that proving energy is required only when you doubt what you believe for yourself? If I had to prove that I truly desired to not have children, then I would have to ask myself why I need to prove it. Do I doubt my choice? A person using the proving energy may be doubting what they are choosing for themselves. Someone honouring their choice does not need to prove it to anybody. There is no correct choice, for that would require judgment and take you back to the outside of the circle and the polarity of it—no ease, no potency, and no you; just polarity to react to.

Defending against a negative comment is also an example of putting up barriers. Being in allowance of what is said means lowering your barriers and saying, "It is interesting that you believe that. What else do you believe?" This allows you to drop your barriers and receive everything from everyone. Can you allow what is being said to you without resisting it, ignoring it or trying to prove it? By standing in your strength, you can let the interesting point of view go right through you. That is true allowance, which is true potency.

When there is a judgment projected at us, we put our energetic barriers up thinking this will protect us. Sometimes, this can be labelled as our "fight or flight" mechanism. We do this, consciously or unconsciously, around people who have judged us in the past or whom we suspect may judge us now or in the future. Others sense these energetic barriers, which fuels the judgment. If you can lower your energetic barriers, the judgment goes right through you, and the person is not triggered to defend their judgment. Saying, "Barriers down, barriers down, barriers down" to yourself silently when you sense a judgment about you allows your body and whole being to receive the contribution of energy without adopting a point of view. Saying it three times tells your body and mind to lower the energetic barriers, avoid the "fight or flight" mode, and allow the energy of what was said to you to flow through you rather than stay stuck within you.

You know you are in your head instead of your heart when you have energetic barriers up. When you are in your head, you are defensive; when you are in your heart, it is easier to choose allowance. Which energy do you think is easier to create your life with? Defensiveness or allowance? You can start to ask yourself, "If I was not thinking (trying to justify) right now, what would I choose?" or, "If I were not defending my point of view right now, what would I choose?" These questions allow you to lower your energetic barriers and be in the present moment to make more conscious choices. This helps to put you in action mode, instead of reaction mode. Living in action mode allows you to be present in your life and create more of what you desire. Are you ready to live your life in action mode, or are you addicted to living your life in reaction mode?

I remember the experience of someone judging me and my agreeing with them, having no point of view, and how this deactivated the person's fight against me. Many years ago, while at work as a firefighter, I was having a conversation regarding energy healing with my co-workers. I was in the moment, barriers down, and with no point of view—meaning I was not attached to persuading them to believe what I was saying. I was truly enjoying the conversation. A co-worker who was usually mean to me said, "Robin, you are such a voodoo doctor!" "Yes, I am!" I smiled. It was amazing to stay present, in the moment, and watch his energy for a fight deflate and to see him walk away bewildered. By my staying in my strength (the centre of the circle with no point of view) with my energetic barriers down, and allowing him to express his judgment, there was nothing for him to fight against. He did not know what to say or do after I totally received his judgment. I had no point of view about that either. I know that to some people, I do act like a voodoo Doctor so I am willing to embrace that energy of being a voodoo Doctor. What judgment could you acknowledge now so you do not have to allow yourself to be controlled by that judgment? Are you willing to stay in the moment, barriers down, and speak with no attachment to outcome? Are you willing to receive a negative judgment with no point of view?

Become Undefinable and Choosing Beyond the Circle

You have learned from the circle theory that when you put yourself in the center of the circle, the judgements coming at you from the outsides are all just interesting points of view of you or definitions of you. You know a definition is just one aspect of you and thus limiting.

You might be saying, "But, Robin, I have spent my entire life trying to define who I am! I have been taught from a young age to discover who I am and define it." Being who you are and having a definition of yourself are two totally separate things, my friend. Being you is just that! There is no definition. You do not fit in a box or within limitations. You are constantly choosing what works for you at any moment, every day! One moment you could choose to be a bitch, and the next you are choosing to perform community service at your local soup kitchen. To do what brings you joy is not to do what others think brings you joy or what you think should bring you joy because others find joy in it. Others may define me as an unmarried woman with no children, but that is their definition. I am a woman who can choose to be (or not to be) anything in this moment. Defining myself requires a constriction of being. Even identifying as a woman can be a limitation. I am a being with no point of view and nothing to prove. Are you able to be you and have nothing to prove? Being you is an energy that does not require definition and is open for any possibility.

The circle is all about explaining how judgment is just an interesting perspective of something. It gives you a visualization of how judgment is created, and that it is about controlling someone or something. Judgment is not about empowerment; it is a limitation of what is possible. Judgment is not about keeping you safe, although over the years we were taught to judge others so we could be safe. Your goal in life is to step out of judgment. Step out of the confines of what judgment is and choose what works for you, what makes you lighter, energetically lighter. Be aware that your choices will always have consequences and be prepared to deal with that. There is an equal amount of good in something as there is bad. There can be so many different perspectives on any given item, person, or situation. It all comes down to a question of what you desire to choose; of choosing something for the pure joy of it, not because it is the right choice or the wrong choice—it is just a choice. As you step into this empowerment, life gets clearer and not clouded by judgment.

When you choose what you desire, you do not have to enter the polarity of any situation. The polarity creates a roller coaster of emotions. The thing is, the roller coaster of emotions can also make you feel more alive, so much so that we can unconsciously be trying to create that polarity to make our lives more interesting, living off judgment and the trauma and drama; pain is a great motivator after all. But this is also what keeps us in those loops, always feeling like we are dealing with the same problems or conflicts. It is when we can step out of judgment and go beyond the trauma and drama where we really get in touch with what we truly desire. Once you can truly embrace yourself and be in allowance, the judgment, the trauma and drama and even the theory of the circle are no longer required. You will be able to choose what works for you, step out of the seemingly endless struggle and not have to judge anyone or anything again. You go beyond the circle, beyond judgment and choose to be you without justification or reasons.

Once you choose you, anything is possible.

Mind, Body, Soul, and Spirit

I believe that we are made up of mind, body, soul, and spirit and these are gateways to help us understand ourselves. Gaining clarity about the four main aspects of me, created a greater understanding of who I am and how to connect to them. I feel I would have created less turmoil in my life if I had this knowledge when I was coming into adulthood. Being clear in my mind with these four main aspects of myself, I can consciously connect to each of them. This clarity made it easier to choose which activity would help me nurture each aspect. Once we perceive them as individual parts forming a whole, we can create the harmony that may be lacking in our lives.

We frequently hear people mention "mind, body, and spirit" or "mind, body, and soul." Is there really a difference between spirit and soul? I believe there is. Soul is the aspect of us that connects us to something outside of us. Spirit is the essences of us, the part of us that makes us unique. I believe that we require individuation of our mind, our body, our soul, and our spirit to live our lives to the fullest. We need to actively nurture all four of the aspects to connect with every element of ourselves. When we do not nurture or connect with them all, this may lead to depression and a sense of feeling lost. Are you willing to connect with your mind, body, soul and spirit?

Mind

We have a mind (a.k.a. our brain), which reminds us to pay our bills, solve our problems, make our "pros and cons" lists, and so on. Your mind must be nurtured daily to keep it healthy and happy and so that it can be depended upon to do what it is required. Your mind is like a calculator that is about comparing the past with the future and making sure you do not forget anything. It is meant to gather information on a subject and put it on the "right or wrong" list. It is not meant to think outside the box or create greater possibilities. I believe too many of us are relying on the mind to make decisions without consulting our hearts enough and listening to our gut instincts. Fun is not created in the mind. Fun is created in the heart, in the core of our being, which is joyful when all four aspects of ourselves are nourished and cared for. Fun is what brings enjoyment to our lives. Possibilities are not created in the mind. The mind can think only of what it has heard, read, or experienced. The mind also loves to live with conclusions and definitions, which are different energies than the energy of possibility. To quote a mental health campaigner, comedian and author, Ruby Wax; "Your brain is designed to keep you alive. It does not give a shit about your happiness."

The mind is a tool to be used and set aside when not in use. You can even exercise and reward it by giving it puzzles and problem-solving activities to tackle, but it does not make the decisions on its own. It is analogous to a car; you use a car to get you to work, then park it and not use it until it is required again. The car helps you get there, but it is not directing the way, *you* are. It requires maintenance and up-keep to continue to get you where you desire to go. What are you doing daily to nurture your mind? Honour it when it comes up with the "pros and cons" list. Say "thank you" to it when it allows you to be totally aware while driving—but do not let go of the wheel and allow it to take you wherever it will!

Are you living your whole life in your brain? If you are using judgment, you are allowing your mind to control your life. Are you willing to honour your mind and not make it wrong when it does what it is best at? What could you do today that would nurture your mind?

To live in a more expansive way, use your mind to complete complex mental tasks and thank it for doing so, but incorporate your whole being into creating your life; this is much more rewarding than using just your mind. What does that mean? It means paying attention to the other parts of you when it is time to make choices and decisions. Yes, you have made a mental list of all the reasons you should logically take that new job, or move across the country, or marry that person, but how does your body *feel* when you consider that prospect? What is your gut telling you? Does it feel light and joyful? Is there a sense of peace that comes over you when you actually allow yourself to imagine stepping into that choice? Are you willing to create your life with your whole being?

Your brain was designed to keep you alive, not worry about whether you are happy or not. Happiness is created when you are willing to step beyond your mind and into you without polarity.

Body

Our body is an element of us that requires separate recognition. It should not be lumped together with the rest of us and not acknowledged. The body is believed to have its own consciousness and requires its own unique nurturing for it to thrive. There are many people that ignore what their body desires and make their body exercise with heavy-duty workouts, and then wonder why they are in constant pain. Maybe your body requires going for a nature walk instead. Maybe it does desire a hard workout today but needs you to skip the squats this time. Are you aware that your body has desires for what it would like in its life? I believe that if people asked their body what it desired, they could create a union to work with their body instead of against it. Creating a union with your body is how to create peace and harmony with it while you are on this earthly plain. Are you united with your body?

By starting a conversation with your body and learning the difference between "light" and "heavy" (or "yes" and "no") is one of the first steps to creating this cooperation with your body. Please stand up and take a deep breath and imagine breathing into your lower abdomen. Get present in your body; the lower in your body you can focus your breath, the more you can get into your being and out of your head. Now, say to your body, "Body, show me yes, show me yes, show me yes. Show me what is true, show me true, show me true. Body, show me what is light, show me light, show me light." Notice what changes within your body as you say these things. My chest area becomes light, and I sway forward. You might waver to one side or feel naturally lighter. It could be anything; do not put emphasis on what it is, just notice the difference, and thank your body for showing you. It is fine to pick one word, like "yes," if it creates more of a reaction in your body. Now, while still standing, say to your body, "Body, show me no, show me no, show me no. Body, show me a lie, show me a lie, show me a lie. Body, show me heavy, show me heavy, show me heavy." Did you notice your body change? Does it feel different from when you asked it to show you lightness and truth? My buttocks get heavy, and I waver backwards. Some people feel their shoulders get heavy. Again, it could be anything for you. Just notice and acknowledge the feeling and thank your body for showing you.

If you do not sense anything in your body, that is totally fine. Before I started alternative therapy practices, I could not even sense what my gut feeling was in response to a question. The more you are willing to get in touch with and honour your body, the more your body will show you a difference between light and heavy, or yes and no. I recommend a BodyTalk session, Access Bars session, or any other alternative body session to help get rid of past stress that may be locked into your body. Are you willing to create a more intimate connection with your body?

Try asking your body what it wishes to eat, who it desires to sleep with, how it wants to move and for how long, etc., and notice the subtle changes that begin to happen. In turn, how does that make your whole being feel? Put your body in the center of the circle, see its many different aspects, and pay attention to those aspects. Your body may wish to move and stretch and be one with nature. Did you know taking a deep breath is like giving your body an internal hug? Are you hugging your body enough? Your goal is to create and nurture a friendship with your body. Once you create this friendship, you will be more likely to honour it and not force it do something against its will. You will receive the benefits of honouring your body and giving it what it truly desires. Creating and nurturing this connection with our body allows us to hear its whispers when something is going on deep inside of it. Your body is a miraculous healing machine; creating a union with it helps to create peace and harmony. What would your life be like if you created a union with your body? Do you desire to be with your body? What is preventing that? What could you do today to create more peace and harmony with your body?

I know a woman who is in constant in pain. One day, I started asking her questions and learned there was a complete lack of nurturing for her body. She would ask her body if it wished to wear high-heeled shoes. Most of the time it would tell her, "No," but she would wear them anyway; her back and hamstrings would be in such pain the next day she could barely move. Unwilling to honour her body and what it desired, she created pain and anguish for herself. I wonder, if she ever chooses to honour her body, would that reduce her pain?

After learning that my body has its own awareness, I started tapping into it daily to see what it desired for the day. When I ask my body what it desires to wear for a day of teaching, it is sometimes amazing what it picks; when I choose what my body desires to wear, I receive a lot of compliments that day. My body lights up with these compliments.

I created a course called "Insights to Your Body Imbalances" (visit www.robinchant.com for more info). The course examines the whispers of what our aches and pains are saying to us. It is about listening to what the body desires and for us to look at our lives where our lack of harmony is creating this pain in our bodies. I have taken this information and applied it to all aspect of my life with my body. I always make and serve popcorn when I teach courses, which is often, and my body started to show symptoms of allergies to the popcorn; I was starting to get hives and other symptoms after eating. So, instead of going into the wrongness of how my body was allergic to the popcorn, I started to ask it what it desired. My body let me know that if I would take breaks from eating popcorn, I would be able to eat it with no allergic reactions. I now go days and weeks without eating popcorn and my body shows no more signs of allergic reactions. I do not recommend this to someone with anaphylactic allergies; however, if you notice your body starting to not enjoy a certain food, get in touch with your body and see if you can create beyond this possible allergy. Are you willing to be gentle with your body and listen to what it is telling you? Are you willing to create a union with your body and be best friends with your body?

Soul

I believe the soul is our connection to something greater, something bigger than us that guides and protects us. Our soul could be connected to God, or a higher deity or Source, or the universe as a whole. The soul is the immortal part of the human, the part that continues on when our body reaches the end of its life. What does it mean to nurture our soul? Your connection to your soul is as unique as your fingerprint, and how you make that connection to it is unique too. Your soul is the being that allows the divine in you to live in this world. (This discussion may not be for those that do not believe in a higher self or life after death.)

Just honouring yourself may be all the soul requires, or it may need more; tapping into your soul daily and listening to its guidance may be needed for it to feel nurtured. This can be done by meditating every day or praying by yourself or with a group; the soul's needs may change daily. When you quiet the mind, it is easier to hear the whispers of your soul. The soul is concerned only with who you are outside of this reality; time is not a concept. It is concerned with evolving and gaining wisdom as one goes through life. Your soul could be thought of as your "wisdom holder"; one would want wisdom to be evolving as we evolve through this lifetime. What could you incorporate into your daily life that would nurture your soul? Whatever this is for you, allow it to be a part of your routine, like brushing your teeth.

Spirit

Now, the fourth aspect that I would like to add is spirit, the essence of who you are. Most people stop at three aspects of you, but I believe you have four distinct parts that make you uniquely yourself. You can not define every aspect of your spirit. When you say you are competitive, you are talking more about the energy of competition than the energy of you. What are you doing daily to nurture your spirit, your essence, your uniqueness? Your uniqueness cannot be duplicated. Are you taking yourself for a walk-in nature if that is what your spirit desires; are you enjoying coffee with a friend; painting; hiking? Doing the things that make your spirit soar—in other words, enjoying life. Your spirit may not be used to having someone listen to it. It may take a while to unite with your spirit, but once you do, you will feel a sense of peace. This sense of peace will spill over into other aspects of you life.

The spirit of someone is what makes them unique. This creates the difference between people; once you start to celebrate your differences, you start to value who and what you are. Your spirit can be ever-changing too. It is like putting your spirit in the center of the circle and seeing every different aspect about it without judgment. The spirit can be made up of many positive and negative aspects, and your task is to enjoy every aspect of being you. Your spirit can evolve like your soul. What you desired at one time to make your spirit smile is probably different twenty years later. Your spirit is the part of you that you want to make best friends with, honour what it desires, and treat it with respect and gratitude. To honour your spirit is basically what makes the inner you smile. Most people know how to have a conversation with another person, and the same ability can be applied to getting to know your spirit. For me, I had to be clear–did I truly desire to not have children, or was that me rebelling against what society desired for everyone? I had to get honest with myself because my decisions affected everyone around me, including me. For many years, I watched adults with children, and I never saw much joy in it. This is not to make anyone wrong—I know people see joy in interacting with children—I am just stating what I was allowing myself to see. I remember being in a restaurant and noticing so much disagreement among families eating together. I knew then, in my spirit, that children were not what I desired to be around twenty four seven. I do know there are magical moments with children; for me, though, it never outweighed the effort I knew it would require.

In a congregation, the priest talks to hundreds of souls; the spirit is what makes each soul unique. So, nurturing your spirit is as unique as you and may change from moment to moment. Creating this union is about being able to realize what the spirit desires and delivering it with ease. Do you know what your spirit desires? Are you willing to connect to your spirit to create more, not only for you but for those around you?

Your mind is what helps you recognize and decipher. Your body is what allows you to feel and receive this earthly experience through its five senses. Your soul is the part of you that lives on, eternally gaining wisdom; and your spirit is the blueprint of unique dreams and desires you come into this life with. And you need all aspects working in harmony to feel whole and complete—to feel like YOU! My invitation to you is to look at these four aspects of yourself and see how you can nurture them and foster their mutual growth.

Gratitude for your body, mind, soul, and spirit is one of the many ways to honour yourself without judgment. When you choose appreciation for each aspect of you, you can stay in the moment and not be in your head judging the past or anticipating the future. This allows each aspect to relax and be present too. By creating a nurturing connection with all four aspects of ourselves we give ourselves and others the gift of us.

Connection

I believe people become dissatisfied with life when they have a loose connection with one or more of these four aspects. If we are unable to create a bond with our body, could that be the basis of our body hurting and causing us pain? If we are unable to create a bond with our mind, does this lead to having diseases that affect the brain somehow? Does it become unreliable and cause us to doubt ourselves? If we are unable to bond with our soul, do we lose our connection to others and our sense of purpose? If we are unable to connect to our spirit, do we lose our love of life?

When I was able to see that there were four very different aspects that make up me, I became more whole. I was treating them all the same. Or maybe more accurately, not treating them at all—not nurturing the different aspects according to what they required. This is what was missing from my life—my connection to my mind, body, soul, and spirit. As I created a connection to and honoured each of them, there became a richness to my life that dissolved any past depression. This has made me wonder if people with depression, or who are feeling lost, have actually lost their connection with their mind, body, soul, and/or spirit. If they could connect with these four aspects, would their depression dissipate?

Johann Hari, a writer and journalist, gave a Ted Talk called, "Everything you think you know about addiction is wrong" (available at www.ted.com/talks/johann_hari_everything_you_think_you_know_about_addiction_is_wrong). Hari shows us that a lack of connection with self and others entices people with drug addictions to continue doing drugs. Hari describes brilliantly the test findings of Vancouver professor Bruce Alexander in the 1970s. He recounts a study in which rats were given two types of water, one normal and one laced with drugs; rats isolated from other rats chose the water laced with drugs and overdosed again and again. The rats that were able to have connections with other rats, almost never drank the drug-laced water and thus avoided overdosing. This shows that when a rat has a connection to others, there is no need to escape life. If humans created more connection within us and with others, would we choose the joy of communion with self and others over the temporary artificial high experienced with drugs and other addictions?

If you do not feel you are connected to your spouse or your friends, this is the time for you to examine how well you are connected to yourself. If you have a lack of connection with yourself, the lack of connection will spill over into other parts of your life. The lack of connection creates inner struggle, leading to struggles with money or relationships or whatever you are desiring to have a connection with. Creating a deeper connection to yourself will allow you to create a deeper connection to other people, or to money, or time, etc. Are you willing to connect to every aspect of yourself and its desires?

How well are you connecting with your mind, body, spirit and soul? Are you willing to create a union to the four main aspects of yourself? Creating a connection to these allows you to create a sense of peace of who you are and this will carry over into your relationships with others.

You can try the following exercise: Sit or stand, calm and relaxed, and ask your mind to show you its energy. Get a sense or an awareness of your mind. It may be very subtle or very obvious, but whatever you are sensing do not make yourself wrong for it. If you do not notice anything, ask it to show you more obviously so that you can understand. Now ask your mind what it requires to be nurtured. The first thing that comes up is the answer; do not question it. It might not make any sense. Just do what it asks. Do the same thing for your body, your soul, and your spirit.

Connecting to yourself is honouring who you are at all times. It is asking questions of yourself and not being attached to the answers. Questions like, "If I were just being me right now, what would I choose?" "If I were being me right now, where would I choose to go?" "If I were being me right now, what would create joy for me?" And just because you hear something like "Running away to a beach in Bali would bring me joy" does not mean you need to drop everything in that moment (though, sometimes that can work too!). But these questions can give you awareness about what may or may not be currently working for you and help you move toward what does. This can change from moment to moment too, that is fine. Allow yourself to be anything in the moment.

How do you connect to each of these different aspects of you? The same way you connect to other people: you ask them questions to get to know them, their likes and dislikes. You can do the same for yourself—ask questions of your mind, body, soul and spirit. Body, what would you like to do today to feel honoured by me?

Do You Value You?

Over the years of seeing many clients and introducing energy healing to many students, there has always been one theme. Clients and students are always saying, "I do not see where I am valuable." They are always looking for all the excuses to not choose themselves and be more. The students will not open a practice and see clients until they see themselves as valuable. They are limiting what they are choosing and they are projecting onto others that they will not be good enough in the sessions. Remember that as you look for how you are valuable, your brain gets busy making a "pro and con" list and telling you everywhere you are valuable and not valuable in your life. This will take you back to the circle; as soon as you start to look for places where you are valuable, the opposite will show up in your life, pointed out either by your own brain or by others. It is the balance of the outside aspects of the circle. As you look at one aspect on one side of the circle you tip the scale for the aspect on the other side to show up too.

You are not meant to look for what is valuable about you; you are meant to value yourself as a being. This is not defining or polarizing anything you say or do as valuable; it is honouring who you truly are. What does that mean? Let me give you an example. Let us pretend your best friend loses everything in a house fire. She hardly gets out with the clothes on her back and is left with no house, no bed, no clothing—nothing. As you open your home for your friend to stay with you, you know you need to be totally there for her. You make sure she has enough blankets, a comfortable bed, and hot food; maybe you would even purchase some new clothing for her. You would go the whole nine yards for your best friend, would you not? Are you willing to be there for yourself in the same capacity? If you choose yes, that is valuing you. Treat yourself as you would treat your best friend. Are you saying things to yourself that you would never dream of saying to a friend? Choose to stop now! Are you willing to take the first step in valuing you? Are you there for you? Are you willing to care for you? Caring means that you can know what you desire and deliver it to yourself. When you value yourself, others and the universe will also see the value in you. Once you choose it for you, it invites others to choose it for you too.

The way you treat yourself invites others to treat you the exact same way. To invite more tenderness into your life, treat yourself with tenderness. To invite more respect, treat yourself with respect. To invite love into your life, love yourself more. It is that simple and all you have to do is choose it.

Some people do not see the value in becoming the truest version of themselves. That is fine; people will choose what they choose. Personally, I was going into a deep depression the further away I got from my connection with my spirit and my body. The more I choose to value me, the more of a connection I have with myself.

In our attempts to seek fulfilment in life, we look to our mentors—parents and people we trust to help us choose. They may say, "Choose what works for you," even when they are unable to show us through example themselves simply because they are not clear with what that means for them. I believe so many people choose what others desire of them so that they do not have to look at what they desire of themselves. Most people do want you to choose what works for you so they can see if they might also choose that. I notice a lot of people will state ideas to others as a way of stating those ideas to themselves. They suggest a way of being to someone else, but what they are really doing is suggesting it to themselves. If you were not treated fairly growing up, I invite you to start treating yourself they way you should have been treated. Choosing to treat yourself with honour and allowance is the first step of letting go of the childhood hurts and becoming more of who you are meant to become. This creates freedom so you are no longer reacting to what is said to you nor what is said about you. You are able to be you without a justification and choose what works for you in any given moment.

I have always had this funny little version of when someone dies, I imagine it goes something like this: they approach the pearly white gates of heaven and are asked, "Did you choose you?" I think a lot of people will respond, "I did this," and, "I did that," describing noble acts toward society, such as volunteering and giving to others. But God or his representative would ask, "But did you choose you? Did you honour and value yourself by staying true to yourself?" I know a lot of people would be at a lost to answer that. Having this as my version allows me to question daily, am I choosing to be me or am I choosing to be what everyone else thinks is me? This is my interesting point of view; we are all born unique, and we nurture this uniqueness by choosing to be our authentic selves and what we truly desire. Are you willing to discover what works for you? Are you willing to discover your uniqueness and honour that?

My Gift to You

My gift to you is to invite you to take what you have read in this book and apply it to your life. Choose to go beyond judgment; choose what works for you; discover what you truly desire. Allow this to become an art for you that you can nurture through your day and life. As you step into the strength of you, you may lose friends; they are people that are addicted to their trauma and drama (the polarity that judgment creates in our lives), and when you do not buy into it, they may not keep you as a friend. When you choose to go beyond the trauma and drama, life opens more possibilities for you, but it may not show up as you would like. Keep your life open to possibilities by living in the power of the question. Remember to use the circle to begin to see other perspectives of anything, anyone, and everything. Allow judgment, whether positive or negative, to flow through you and be a gift to you.

Discover and nurture the four major aspects of you—your mind, your body, your soul, and your spirit. Choose yourself without judgment, without conclusion, with an open way of being, and in total allowance. Once you choose yourself, anything and everything is possible. Allow this new way of being—choosing yourself—to be the paint you use in the art of your life.

Are you painting the canvas of your life with judgments or with possibilities? Each is a choice; one will constrict your life and the other with expand your life.

Acknowledgements

First, I wish to thank you for choosing more, for choosing to go beyond your current position. It takes strength and courage to choose something for yourself. Deep in our hearts, we all know that we can choose to live our lives differently, stepping beyond judgment and into our strength. I am inviting you to the art of choosing you.

I am eternally grateful to the many clients who came to see me for sessions many years ago, who were looking for more ways to heal, grow, and be themselves through the stresses of life. I thank them from the bottom of my heart, for the more they learned about themselves, the more I, too, was able to learn, grow, and be myself with total ease.

My gratitude extends to the many students I have inspired over the years to look at their lives and create tools to aid themselves and others on their journeys.

Many people created space as I was writing this book, men and women who invited me to new discoveries. My heart has so much gratitude for the amazing beings who contributed their insights, rewording the passages in the book. Special thanks go to Helen, Jacqueline, Julie, Betty Anne, and Gary. Without these writing coaches, this book would not have been created. Helena, you are an inspiration to me for you knew what I was trying to convey in this book and words cannot express the acknowledgment you deserve. I am truly thankful that you collaborated with me to create this guide to self-discovery. My heart fills every time I go to thank you.

Finally, to Gary Douglas, who founded Access Consciousness™, and his co-creator Dr. Dain Heer, I cannot express my gratitude adequately. You showed me parts of myself that I was unable to acknowledge at that time. You inspire me to choose more for me, just as you inspire others to choose more for themselves. You helped me see that stepping beyond judgment is how I am finally able to choose for myself. This book is dedicated to you and to the ones who desire more of themselves in their own lives.

Appendix A
Using the Circle

One of the greatest gifts you can gift to yourself is to be present with you and what really drives you—to be there for you without judgment and in total allowance. Are you willing to be present with you? If there is judgment that triggers you, to be in total allowance requires you to release the emotional charge around that judgment. Having no emotional charge around either that word or its opposite creates total choice in your life.

There are many modalities that are all about releasing old emotions; please choose the ones that you are drawn to. I have created a course called "The Art of Choosing You," which is all about dissipating emotional charges and receiving more of you.

Let us take an issue that upsets you, like not being heard. Perhaps your partner is not hearing what you are saying. Take the judgment "not being heard," and ask yourself, "What are the negative aspects of not being heard?" Write down your answers and be willing to let each of them go. Some may require more digging to discover why they have an emotional charge to them. One example could be, "When I was growing up, no one listened to me." This may have led you to become a troublesome child so people would listen to you. Let that go; allow it to dissipate and release from your body and being. Deep breathing is amazingly helpful to allow us to process our trapped emotions. Take a deep breath in, and let go of all the trauma and drama of not being heard when you were younger—you can do this by remembering a moment when you felt not listened to and imagine your grown-up self giving your younger self exactly what was needed but lacking in that moment, and imagine your younger self really receiving that gift. Once you have cleared all the emotional trauma of not being heard, ask yourself, "What is the value of not being heard?" In other words, how might not being heard be serving you in an unconscious way? Allow your answers to seep up, write them down and let go of each one. You may be surprised by what arises. One example could be, "If I am not heard, then no one can see me and judge me." I believe there are a lot of us that deep down do not desire to be heard, for if we are heard, then we could be judged, and we desire to avoid judgment at all costs. Not being heard is keeping us safe. With each answer that comes up for the value of not being heard, allow yourself to let go of all the emotions around that too. So, when you ask yourself, "Am I okay with not being heard?" there should be no emotional charge to it, and when you ask yourself, "Am I okay with being heard by everyone?" there should also be no emotional charge with that either. There could be excitement, and that is fine; with the excitement of what you have to say, the world will listen. We are clearing both sides of the circle of the issue of not being heard so that you can create a life of total choice.

The moral of this little tool is to also ask if *you* hear yourself. So, being upset at not being heard is directly related to you not hearing yourself. Every trigger or judgment is related to the opposite judgment and then related to you and whether you are that trigger or judgment to yourself. Once you start to listen to yourself and the four aspects of you—mind, body, soul, and spirit—there will likely be fewer times in your life that others do not listen to you.

This is just a taste of the tools that are available to you; my classes are about helping you to be able to receive any aspect of you to create your life with. For example, are you able to receive that you are *not* valuable in life? Are you able to receive that energy so you are not constantly reacting to someone saying you are not valuable in their life? Playing with these tools allows you to receive everything in life and allows you to choose what creates your life greater.

Appendix B

Listing of various Alternative Therapies & reference material:

Access Consciousness https://www.accessconsciousness.com/

BodyTalk https://www.bodytalksystem.com/

Reiki www.reiki.org

The Art of Choosing You – www.artofchoosingyou.com – this is where more books can be purchased and there is information on bulk orders, buying eBooks, courses to host Robin Chant. Email Robin at robin@artofchoosingyou.com for more details on bulk orders

www.robinchant.com – many classes and workshops to choose from

www.thework.com Byron Katie – all about emotional intelligence

www.ted.com – various speakers – especially Jill Bolte Taylor – a stroke of insight & Johann Hari

Books: Excuse me your life is waiting by Lynn Grabhorn

Pragmatic Psychology by Susanna Mittermaier

Being You, Changing the World by Dr. Dain Heer

Appendix C
Summary of the Questions for Ponder & Self Discovery

Am I hiding an essential part of me from others?

Was I honoured for my choices while I was growing up? Do I honour my choices now?

Are my choices based on what others desire for me?

Am I present with my choices? How could I be more present when I make choices?

Am I allowing myself to get in touch with inner desires or am I allowing my judgment or others to keep me from this?

Am I willing to choose what I actually desire?

Do I judge others when I do not understand their choices?

Do I honour the choices that people make that are close to me?

Who am I?

Am I willing to be me without any definitions?

Do I have a label or definition of me that is limiting me? Am I willing to be me without a definition or judgment? Do I enjoy letting judgments limit me?

What would I choose in my life if judgment was not a factor? What limiting point of view do I have that if I let go of would create something entirely different for me?

Am I willing to have more choices in my life? Am I willing to create more possibilities in my life?

Do I have freedom in creating who I am? Am I stuck and using that as an excuse not to go deeper in who I am?

Am I willing to bring in the peacefulness of nature and have total allowance for myself and others?

Am I willing to live my life in action instead of reaction to every point of view directed at me?

Do I give someone's opinion of me more than one percent of my thoughts? Whose opinion am I making more significant than mine? What or who would I be if I let that go?

Am I willing to let go of judgment of myself that I have held? Am I willing to choose and create beyond my judgments and the judgments of others?

Am I willing to embody any point of view, any energy, if the moment requires it?

Am I willing to step into my potency no matter what others say to me or about me?

How can I use the circle theory to create more in my life?

Am I willing to sit in the energy of what else is possible here or am I addicted to know conclusions and decisions? Do I enjoy having a predictable life?

If I was not thinking right now or trying to justify my choices, what would I choose?

Am I willing to lower my energetic barriers and be more of me? Am I willing to live in the present moment with no barriers on how life should me?

Am I willing to receive a negative judgment of me with no point of view?

What could I choose today that would create an intimate connection with my body, mind, spirit and soul? Am I willing to see that those are four individual aspects of me and together they create a whole?

Am I willing to nurture my mind, body, soul and spirit individually and daily?

What could I choose today that would allow me to step beyond judgment?

Printed in Canada